S T O L E N

S O U L

by

B E R N A R D   H O L S T E I N

First published in Australia in 2004 by Judy Shorrock
Distributed by UWA Press

Copyright Bernard Holstein 2004

Typeset in Western Australia
Printed by Optima Press, Osborne Park, Western Australia

ISBN 0-646-43446-2

Bernard Holstein was born in a small German hamlet in

County Holstein, now part of Schleswig-Holstein.

His parents farmed a portion of land and tended

a small vineyard with Jochim and Miriam Weissmantel,

Magda's parents. Bernard was very close to his

brother Peiter and his cousins Rachel and Leah.

The extended family numbered 44.

In the summer of 1943, they were taken away by

trucks and train to Auschwitz Birkenau.

Of the 44 members of his family, only Bernard was

selected to go right instead of left,

and was the only one to survive.

This book is dedicated to the memory of more than
1.5 million children who were snatched from
the playgrounds of Europe and destroyed
in gas chambers and crematoria by
the Third Reich

ACKNOWLEDGEMENTS

To my wife, Dee, my never ending thanks for your support.

To my fine friends Judy, Joanne and Kim, my sincere appreciation.

I was sterilised in 1944 as part of an experiment by the German Army, but I have two adopted children, three step-children and grandchildren. My eldest daughter, Michelle, always wanted me to put my experience of Auschwitz into words so that I could share them with the world. This book is the beginning of that story - thank you, Michelle.

I remember the two families on the North Coast of New South Wales who took me in and cared for me in those first trying years when it seemed almost impossible that my life would ever be normal again. Later, when schooling was over for most, the Catholic Church put me in a boarding school to help me with my secondary education. Such acts of kindness will never be forgotten.

I thank God for caring for me with His Love
that knows no bounds.
Baruch Hashem

Leviticus Fire

Leviticus fire, Auschwitz burning
God of Salvation, calling His children,
Calling them home.
Angels flying all around, waiting
Children in Auschwitz's ovens burning
Being refined as pure as gold
Father at Heaven's gate waiting
Messiah's arms outstretched and crying
Angels' mansions showing
Children around God's throne dancing
Erhardt and Mikhail with two million children's voices
Chorus leading

Bernard Holstein

Always remembered, never forgotten,
my two fond friends
Erhardt and Mikhail.

As members of the Underground in Auschwitz-Birkenau,
we did deeds that, had we been caught, would have
seen us hanged or shot in the back of the head.

I salute you, my friends.

Prelude

How do we really know the truth? Memory is mutable, truth illusive. We present facts through the distortions of time and the subjective mirror. History, it has been shown, is far from benign; it is a powerful tool of ideology, fashioned by notions of nationalism and other grand narratives. I know of some facts that cannot be disputed. Auschwitz existed, so did the ovens and the gas chambers, they are still there for anyone to see. I know because I was there, I have the numbers tattooed on my left forearm to prove it. I know that I came from a world seeped in culture and traditions that no longer exist. I know that there is a fire burning within me and that the man my father wanted me to be has been sacrificed upon that fire. I know it is the fire of the righteous, and the sacrifice is the sacrifice of the purest of the pure.

The ovens that burnt the children of Israel burnt with the passion of Leviticus. The very best were sacrificed there; those who survived did so to let the world know that the light of the Jewish people will never be extinguished. I survived to tell a tale of cunning and friendship, of humanity in the face of the inhumane, a tale of bravery and courage and incredible risk. I survived to tell the story of a modern day sacrificial offering that triggered the creation of a Jewish state. In Leviticus it states that only the best is good enough for sacrifice, it is the ultimate price for the ultimate prize. Never again will the children of Israel be that vulnerable, never again will the children of Israel be at the mercy of others.

ONE

I HAD THAT DREAM AGAIN LAST NIGHT. I was watching you drown. You were trapped beneath other bodies, staring at me from under the water with your eyes wide open, and somehow, as is only possible in dreams, I was on the outside, helplessly watching you, and I felt the fear and the horror again, those old familiar sensations: the charge of adrenaline like an electric shock that ripples hotly through the body, cold sweat, heart pumping, the heat of fear rising up from the stomach into the throat and then the disbelief, the mind's denial that something like this could actually be happening. I didn't scream, I couldn't, I was choking, shaking, and sweating. I looked over to your side of the bed and saw you lying there, startled. "I'm fine, I'm okay, it's just a nightmare. Sorry."

I have dreamt a hundred ways of death. Awake I have witnessed a hundred ways to kill and maim a human being; I have seen the most painful, the slowest, the quickest and the most efficient ways to die. I have been witness to the killing of one and to the slaughter of thousands. I have watched the people I have loved die over and over in my nightmares, and

I awake, clinging to the edge of the bed, believing in the reality of the dream, unable to bring my mind back to you sleeping safely and peacefully next to me, to this warm room, the food in the fridge and the water from the tap. Like a child I cannot separate the nightmare from reality, as a child the nightmare was my reality.

I got out of bed and walked out into a clear tropical night. The sea had trapped the moon and was tossing it gently across its surface. I breathed in the warm night air, tasting the salt and the unmistakable scent of night. The moon stared at me, a silent witness. I felt its coldness within my chest, a hard cold core where there should be emotions, a tightness that won't allow me to feel pain, joy or sorrow. I feel only that light reflected from others. This is the same moon that shone down on the camps, silent witness to the brutality of a regime steadfast in its belief in its own superiority, its legitimacy over others. The same moon that watched over the killings in Auschwitz, in Dachau, in Treblinka and has since been witness to slaughter in Vietnam, in Ethiopia, in Chechnya.

I hate that moon staring mercilessly down, passive. I hate it because, like me, it is trapped within a role it must play, forced to reflect the glory of the sun. Ensnared by the earth's gravitational pull it journeys on a predetermined course. It is what it is, it cannot be anything else and I am a Jew, I cannot be anything else. Sometimes the label is dirty Jew: how loathsome it is to be something despised, something less than human in the eyes of another. I feel my Jewishness exposed even though for years I have tried to hide behind a mask of conformity. I worked hard at adopting an Australian accent, Australian mannerisms, I worked hard at hiding my past, my difference, my shame. But I cannot escape my nightmares. The fear paralyses me, the horror resurfaces, the pain returns to haunt me over and over again. I scream in my sleep and wake drenched in sweat and shaking like a leaf. "What is it? What are you dreaming about that makes you scream so loud?" ask my roommates, my lovers, my wife. "It's nothing," I reply, "just a bad dream. I'm sorry I woke you, go back to sleep."

For years now I have hidden the telltale numbers tattooed on my left forearm, shamed by their presence, not wanting people to know where I have been, what I have seen, what a pitiful creature I truly am. I have worked in remote places, trying to escape my past, trying to escape my terror, trying to escape...

It seemed to work for a while. I lived a lie, but I lived. Until fate stepped in.

I was working as a chef on a remote island off the north coast of Western Australia when a backpacker happened by and triggered a memory that set in motion a journey into the past. Jürgen Albrecht was a few years younger than I, having been born in the late forties. He was an inquisitive man. I had noticed him because he seemed to examine everything, going about with his camera and taking notes, never sitting still for a moment. He appeared to run on pure energy. I overheard him saying that he was a doctor, recently retired, and was now spending his leisure time travelling the globe. A tall, thin, fair man with deep set blue eyes, he had a way of speaking that was so painfully familiar. A turn of phrase or a gesture, something triggered a memory deep within. I knew he was German before he confirmed it. It wasn't until his last day on the island that I summoned enough courage to talk to him.

He said there were still some photos he wanted to get before he left. He said he was German and I said I was too, a long,

long time ago. We began talking and I told him I was from County Holstein, right up north.

"Is it still as nice and green as it used to be?" I asked

"I was there once on holiday," Jürgen said, "ja, it's very green. Tell me, how is it that you used to live up there?"

"I used to live there with my parents," I explained, "and then we were all taken to Auschwitz and after that I came to Australia."

"I'm very sorry."

"Don't worry about it, it all happened a long time ago." I said dismissively.

But he wanted to talk more, perhaps he was homesick or lonely, perhaps he was just curious. I asked him if he would like some breakfast, but he declined saying he would prefer to go outside and talk. We walked onto the veranda outside the dining area and sat on the low brick wall over-looking the ocean.

"I am so very sorry you were in Auschwitz," he said. "I went through Poland recently and visited Auschwitz. I just cried and cried."

"It's over now," I said, shifting uncomfortably.

For a while we sat enveloped in silence, suffocating in the shame of the past, each occupied by his own thoughts.

Finally Jürgen broke the silence: "Do you think you can find it in your heart to forgive me for what we have done to you?" he asked choking on the disgrace of a nation. I stared, surprised. He had no part in Hitler's Final Solution and yet I realised that he carried the guilt of his fathers in the same place I carried my shame, so deep within, so ingrained in his being. I thought of the pain of his generation, the remorse and the burden borne by so many and recognised my own pain and loss. And yet if I said no, where would that leave him? But if I said yes, then I knew that we would both have a chance of coming to terms with our lives. I believed then and I believe now that the bitterness we carry will kill us far more effectively than Hitler ever could.

So I replied, "It is not for me to forgive you, but for us both to find forgiveness within ourselves."

He hugged me and in that simple moment of shared understanding and forgiveness the wall I had built so many years before to protect that nine year-old boy began to crumble and we cried, him for his inherited guilt, and me, I cried for the very first time in nearly 60 years. I cried for Benoni, the little boy buried so deep within me, confused and frightened and so very alone. I cried for the life I had lost, for the family and friends I would never see again, I cried for the country I had once loved, I cried for the man I was never going to be and the children I was never going to have.

We talked for hours as the sun heated the air around us, sitting on the wide veranda of the guesthouse. We talked about God, about faith, about hatred. He told me of his youth and of his travels, and I told him of my life in Australia. We talked about Auschwitz, about the rise of Nazism, about the annihilation of a culture, and I began to think about my past, about who I was and what I had become and I was reminded of a promise I had once made to record what I had seen and been through in Auschwitz. Jürgen reminded me of this promise.

"Bernie," he said, "there will come a time when there is no one left to speak of what happened. In twenty years, there will be no more living survivors. You've got to sit down now and write this, tell it so the world can see. You should tell your story before it is too late."

In Judaism we are exhorted time and time again to remember and so we tell our children and grandchildren stories: the stories of Pesach, Purim and Chanukah, the stories of Abraham, Isaac and Jacob, of Sarah, Rebecca and Rachel. These stories get repeated throughout the generations and the context that the story is told in becomes a part of the story, infusing it with meaning. And yet how do you speak of the unspeakable, how do you tell your children of the awfulness of Auschwitz, what context is benign enough to enable such stories to be told? Our language does not provide us with the necessary words to speak of such horror; so many stories are trapped in silence. One story told embodies the stories of seven others that cannot be told, remembers those seven who did not survive, ensures that something of their legacy lives on, a reminder of their existence. They did not die for nothing, even though it may have seemed that the world had been drained of all meaning, all humanity, that everything they valued, their dignity, their families, their culture, had been invalidated. Their voices shatter sleep, screaming to be heard, night after night in dreams of carts, trains and death. I have kept these voices to myself for so long, not telling anybody about who I am, what happened to me, where I came from. Those voices remain trapped, screaming to be heard, the voices of a million children whose childhood ended so abruptly, the voices of the innocent, of the pure.

After I have gone, who will remember the three boys who, with the courage and daring possessed only by the young, managed to rise above the horrors perpetrated upon them, managed to hold on to their humanity and their faith, their spirit and their humour, and who in their own way managed to fight back? I can't hold onto anything anymore. It is time to tell my story so that the others who can no longer speak will be remembered.

Two

I HAD THE MISFORTUNE of being born at a time when the world was dominated by Hitler and the Third Reich. My family was proudly German. Their only crime, and one they would die for, was the fact that they were Jewish. Who was I before Auschwitz? I must confess that I remember very little. I only know what I became there and that it defined the adult I am today. Would I have tended the vines as my father and grandfather did in the gentle and fertile Holstein County, or would I have blazed with passion and fervour in the newly created State of Israel? These are questions I cannot answer for I no longer know who that boy was. Instead, I became a thief, a liar, and a saboteur. I became hard, unable to either feel or express real emotion, a landless misfit, without family, identity or country. And yet I never once, in those years of hell and the very many wilderness years that followed, lost either my belief in humanity or my passion for life. And that miracle, for indeed it is a miracle, was brought about through an association with two boys, Erhardt and Mikhail, who were to save my life in many ways, who taught me how to fight back, who believed in me and looked out for me, and in whom

I found meaning when our very existence was meaningless.

I was always tall for my age, and strong from playing in the vineyards while my father and uncles laboured. It was man's work, tending the vines, picking the grapes, pressing and sorting, and my cousins and I used to long for the day we would be included in the mystical process that turns the sweet white grapes into a clear, crisp wine. We would run through the rows of vines, playing catch or hide and seek, in anticipation of one day being called upon and initiated into the games of men. I do not doubt that we were annoying. We were constantly underfoot, shouting and calling to one another, tripping over spikes and getting tangled in the vines. But perhaps the sweet air and the gentle sun warming the grapes soothed the tempers of the men and their mild chastisements failed to dampen our spirits or curb our enthusiasm.

I remember family evenings: the chill in the rest of the house sharply contrasted by the warmth of the stove radiating heat through the kitchen. We would all gather after dinner in the alcove surrounding the stove and I, sleepy but reluctant to leave the warmth of the kitchen, would curl up in the arms of my mother while my father placed a large jar of money on the white painted table. "Don't mark my table," my mother would admonish sternly as he and my grandfather began to count the day's takings.

The conversations around the fire in the alcove of the kitchen became increasingly disturbing. Sleepy, nestled in the crook of my mother's arm, my stomach full and my senses suffused with the sounds and smells of Shabbat, I heard soft talk of rising anti-Semitism, of disappearing Jews, I heard Palestine mentioned, visas and quotas. I listened as raised voices debated the possibilities and impossibilities of emigration, unless of course the soldiers were there, then the evening was filled with praise for our glorious fatherland and the drunken singing of German national songs.

The soldiers had appeared quite suddenly in the village but did not really disturb our lives at first. I remember coming home from school one day and seeing a soldier sitting at our kitchen table. I asked my mother what was going on.

"Hush, Benoni, don't say anything," she said, " I'll explain later. He is going to spend some time with us."

There had been a lot of soldiers around, but now they were to be billeted in our homes and we were to be host to one of them at a time.

The soldiers became a part of our household; some were polite, others not, but they always seemed stern and my brother Peiter and I were more than a little frightened of them. At first it had been quite pleasant, they were strange guests, but still guests, and treated us well and with respect. Other than having to watch what was said, they seemed to be just one more inconvenience of the war. However, their presence was not to remain benign, they became more demanding, less respectful, and I watched helplessly as my father seethed and my mother bit her lip as their requests turned into demands. Hitler's war machine was gaining strength, the Final Solution was being ratified, and the soldiers no longer had to contain their distaste for Jews. They began to wear their superiority proudly.

The changes happened slowly at first. The army requisitioned the old synagogue and services became more discreet. As children we didn't really mind, the services were long and tedious and we would much rather have been running around outside anyway. Ironically, we associated our new-found freedom with the arrival of the soldiers. We accepted their presence with the simplicity of children, like blackouts in the evenings and food rationing; they were just another manifestation of war. We thought we were useful to the Third Reich, we represented the glorious Aryan way of life, we worked, we produced good grapes and wine, we minded our business. But then one day, a simple day like any other, the trucks rolled in with soldiers carrying rifles.

As always, my grandfather had picked up Peiter, myself and our cousins, Rachel and Leah, from school. He had come straight from the fields; still with the smell of the earth on his skin. He drove a cart led by an old farting nag with a gentle disposition that matched my grandfather's. We loved that horse almost as much as we loved him, screaming with laughter every time she farted, teasing each other mercilessly over the origin of the smell. Clamouring down to open and shut gates, fighting over whose turn it was, it seemed to be a day just like any other day, until we saw the soldiers.

"Don't be frightened, I'll talk to them," said my grandfather as he slowly climbed down from the cart.

"Get your things together, there is a truck waiting. You are to go on the truck."

There was nothing more to be said, no more questions were tolerated. My grandfather hurried towards the house, his drawn face silencing our questions. There, my parents and grandmother were waiting, tense and pale.

We were loaded onto those trucks, there had been a mad scramble to get anything we could take with us. We had never seen any weapons before and were frightened by the sight of them. We were hurried on, prodded by rifles, shouted at; there was no time to think. The nightmare had begun.

In the cattle transport the air was far from sweet. About a hundred hot and sweaty bodies pressed together and the overriding smell of fear. Fear stinks. Animals can smell it immediately; the German dogs at the station smelt it on each and every Jew and growled their supremacy. The soldiers ignored it; they had their orders, to get these Jews on the trains as quickly and efficiently as possible. So few carriages for so many people, never mind, just squash the last batch in. We can't sit, we can't stand, there are elderly, where's the water, the facilities, this is inhuman.....The soldiers shrug, it's the war, we all have to make sacrifices, you are going to help in the factories, that is to be your part in the war effort.

"It's for the fatherland," my father says to comfort my elderly grandparents, Miriam and Jochim Weissmantel. How they loved him, this tall, proud son-in-law of theirs. He had swept their daughter off her feet, with his fair hair, broad shoulders and sky-blue eyes. He was so German, so unlike the pale Yiddishe boys in their black gabardine, who spent all their time indoors studying Torah. He was tall and strong and robust. He gave them all a sense of being part of Germany, rather than part of an alienated sub-culture despised by all in Europe, suffering pogroms, discrimination, speaking a language neither Hebrew nor German.

Yet, they could not escape their heritage and I remember my mother wearing her yellow star with defiance, saw her pain and embarrassment when she walked past a shop sign announcing that they would not serve Jews. They were inescapably Jewish, disempowered by the machinations of the Nazi regime.

"If this is our contribution so be it," they say as they resign themselves to the discomfort of the open truck that is to take us to the station, adjusting their bundles of possessions to provide some comfort. My father tried to position us so that we would have some protection from the sun and wind.

Staunchly proud of being German, he turned a blind eye to what must have been painfully obvious. They consider us a threat to the war he muses, and want us placed somewhere safe. He had heard about Kristallnacht;, he had heard about Jews disappearing, being arrested and never heard of again; he had heard of kidnappings and bribery; he had heard about the ghettos and the confiscation of businesses; but he reasoned that these were city problems and city people can be troublemakers, they can stir up anti-Semitic sentiment.

It was no secret that the Jews were despised in Europe, had suffered persecution and acts of blatant anti-Semitism for as long as they had resided in Europe. It was part of his cultural heritage, he understood it, expected it. He was used to being a scapegoat, blamed for all the troubles of the world. Until now, it hadn't really impacted too greatly on his life. He had worked in the fields, he did not miss the company of Gentiles, he surrounded himself with good friends and family. Together they made good wine, the best in the region, so it was to be expected that there was some jealousy, envy even. It was not good to stand out too much, to draw too much attention to yourself.

Perhaps through this contribution, by co-operating in this small way, they would show the world that they are German, first and foremost, that being Jewish and German are not mutually exclusive. Silently he struggled with the conflict. No one seemed to find a conflict in being Christian and German, or Catholic and German, why make such a fuss about the Jews?

That we are never going to be a part of Hitler's great Aryan race is self-evident, but surely there is a role the Jewish people can play in the great Third Reich? We are going to work in the factories after all; we are on our way to make a contribution, to help Germany defend herself, to partake in the building of a great nation. Perhaps that was not what my father truly believed; perhaps that was only what he told me, his eldest son, to soothe my fears, in answer to my endless questions.

We all huddle together on a station platform, people I have grown up with, teachers, Rabbis, neighbours and family. People who have woven the tapestry of my childhood with the bright colours of Purim, with the golden lights of Chanukah, with the deep red of the wine drunk at Pesach. "There are forty-four of us here, forty-four members of our family," notes my mother, straining her head to find familiar faces because the soldiers were not allowing us to move freely on the platform but forcing us to remain in groups.
"Look Peiter" I try to distract my younger brother who is clinging fiercely to my mother's skirts, "There are Rachel and Leah". Peiter raises his head to see our cousins. His face is pale and tear streaked, and I want to make him smile. The ride to the station in the back of an open truck had been long and he was tired and hungry and wanted to go home, and now the barking of the dogs and the shouts of the soldiers were frightening him. I wave at the girls and they wave back. We are a community; we are an entity, something vibrant and strong. Dogs and soldiers with rifles cannot threaten our existence. We will endure and then go back to our lives amid the vines, to weekly Shabbat dinners enfolded in the laughter and love of family and friends, followed by sleepovers - head to toe with cousins in thick mattresses that dip so deeply in the middle you feel as though you will never manage to climb

out. And when you eventually do escape, clamouring up for air, you leave behind a cacophony of shouts and laughter as the others roll fluidly into the middle filling the empty space. Huddled under thick covers, whispering and giggling late into the night, drifting in and out of sleep, safe and warm in our predictable world.

When I think back to those childhood days spent in Northern Germany among thick forests and vines overhanging with fruit, I remember long sunny days filled with warmth, love and laughter, not in the least bit due to the copious amounts of wine drunk at every opportunity, wine of which my father was inordinately proud.

He was tall and imposing and while my brother and I were rather afraid of him, he in turn was rather afraid of my mother. Magda Weissmantel-Holstein was very proud of her family, very gracious and exceptionally loving. She adored her parents who lived on an adjacent farm and shared the workload, helping in the fields or in the house. Like an ancient vine, thick and strong at the base, grounded in the soil, my grandparents and those before them were the strength that held my family together, giving us a sense of purpose, of belonging, of identity. As the vine sees resolution in the dictates of the seasons, so our lives were regulated by the rhythms of Judaism, of Shabbat and the festivals, of kashrut and Torah.

Sometimes a familiar smell will accost me, and I will all too briefly be in my mother's kitchen eating a freshly baked poppy-seed slice; I could always be bribed with a poppy-seed slice. Fragments of a Jewish life left long behind.

My mother was well known for her generosity, and equally for her stubbornness and pride. Everyone who came to visit had to be fed in varying degrees, and never managed to escape without taking a little something home for their family. Her passion for feeding the world was overshadowed only by her fanaticism for cleanliness and personal hygiene.

Our bathtime was a favourite time for her, she took such great pride in seeing us scrubbed and shining, dressed in clean clothes ready for Shabbat. The process of getting there however was pure torture. First the water had to be heated in a huge copper cauldron. This required the lighting of a fire and the fireplaces were, of course, indoors.

Memory is a tricky business, my memories of that time are infused with sunshine, and yet summer was, in fact, relatively short. However, when I remember bathtime, it is always winter; my mother complaining to my father about the damp wood billowing smoke throughout the house, my father muttering under his breath about forces out of his control. What child wants to stop what they are doing, undress in a cold room off the kitchen, in front of their mother or even worse, have themselves undressed by their mother? But then, once immersed in the warm steamy water, why would you ever want to get out? Having been scrubbed and tweaked and rubbed and checked the thought of emerging from the womblike warmth of the tub into the cold often smoky air was decidedly unappealing. Threats of calling my father usually did the trick and I would step out onto a footcloth placed strategically next to the bath to prevent the now clean skin of my feet from coming into contact with anything remotely carrying even the slightest trace of dirt. Towels were separated into one for the face and one for the body. Once more I would be rubbed and tweaked until shivering and, satisfactorily dry, I was finally allowed to dress in the clean, pressed clothing set aside for this occasion. Stiffly formal, longing for the comfort of everyday clothes, terrified of causing pants to crease or shoes to scuff my younger brother, Peiter, and I would stand to attention and be inspected, adjusted, hair combed, shoulders straightened until pronounced fit to see in the Sabbath.

How I longed for those wonderful bathtimes when, trapped in the nightmare of Auschwitz, I found myself covered in sores and lice, mauled by maggots and rats, wearing ill-fitting clothing taken off the body of some poor sod without any hope of ever being washed.

How do you know who you are when there is no-one to confirm your memories? How do you know who you are when you don't have your family around you to provide a framework for your identity? Snatches of conversations remembered, images of places and people shift, fade and transform with each retelling of my story. As an adult I have no touchstone to verify truth. There is no one with whom I can compare notes; I have not revisited the site of my birth, nor the place where my childhood abruptly ended. The ones who could have given my life continuity, filled in the gaps of my memory and given my story shape and clarity, are all dead.

If I remember a school, I remember a boy fidgeting in Maths class, unable to form a relationship with the numbers dancing on the page. Is this a later memory of an adolescent who had come to distrust any and every form of authority including the figures which reduced a human being to a mere statistic? In my mind I think I am at a small Jewish school with maybe 20-30 other children, but is this possible? Surely Jewish schools were closed. Jews were not allowed to attend public German schools, so perhaps it was a makeshift school set up by some of the parents in the area, but who is there left to ask? To whom do I turn to ratify my memories? Our entire community was sent to Auschwitz and I, the only member of my family of forty-four to survive the selection process on the train ramp at Auschwitz, was separated from the other familiar faces partly because of my mother.

My mother was a formidable woman of great strength. When the German soldiers descended on our homes, shouting orders and brandishing their weapons, she kept her calm. When the dogs growled and bared their teeth at the slightest infraction, she kept her calm. Crowded onto the back of a truck with no food or water or facilities, she maintained her dignity ensuring that four-year old Peiter and I were as comfortable as possible. While my father saw to her elderly parents, her concern was for her children. She had supervised the packing of the basic essentials needed for the trip: some warm clothes for even though it was summer, who knew how long we would be away, some food and water for the journey of who knew how many days, perhaps some precious souvenirs, some money or jewellery stitched into the lining of a coat. I can still picture her dressed, in the heat of summer in that great winter coat. Whatever it was, she took care of it, her quiet efficiency allaying our fears.

I remember the shouting and the dogs barking. I remember old men being prodded in the back with rifles to hurry them up, I remember upon our arrival at the station after a day's journey on the back of a truck, my father going up to a group of people he recognised in an attempt to get information. No one seemed to know anything; everyone was frightened, hungry, thirsty and tired. And then there was the train. Rows and rows of carriages used for the transport of cattle, still with the lingering smell of their previous occupants, straw scattered on the floor. Airless, stifling in the summer heat, and yet my mother survived this with dignity and decorum.

The dying, bleeding, shitting, urinating, crying, moaning mass that became our world for what seemed an eternity did not shake my mother's equilibrium. But when we were finally offloaded onto the ramp outside the imposing entrance to the Auschwitz camp, my mother, Magda Weissmantel-Holstein, decided to take a stand.

THREE

ARBEIT MACHT FREI.

Not even in my thoughts do I want to return and yet I cannot forget. It has taken me so long just to be able to confront this event, this one single event that marked the end of my innocence, the start of the nightmare.

It was always to my mother that I looked for strength and guidance, and in my eyes she was indestructible, had all the answers, was always there to make things right. Innocence depends upon the trust a child has in the adults that govern his or her world. The child develops its own strength and confidence from this. The gradual awareness of the frailty of humanity, the knowledge and acceptance of a parent's weakness, these are essential parts of growing up. It is only when we see our parents as not so different from ourselves, as vulnerable and subject to the same capricious laws of the universe, that we finally emerge from the fog of adolescence into adulthood. But what if that realisation is suddenly forced upon a child, how does that child deal with the trauma of a premature immersion into the world of adulthood, moreover into a world dominated by sadism, cruelty and deceit?

I am not the first child to experience this sudden and cruel wrenching from childhood, and, judging from the way of the world, will not be the last. Childhood has no place in a world of violence and sudden loss. As an adult, fully grown and accepted into the world of men, I still carry within me that young boy's pain; it clouds my judgement, strangles my emotions, twists and turns in my gut every time I see a mother and child, every time I try to connect with another human being. There is an integral part of my emotional being that is not fully realised. It is as effective an amputation as the severing of a limb, and similarly one still feels the need to scratch. I am still that boy crying for my mother, wanting to be soothed by her, wanting to be told that everything will turn out just fine, wanting to reclaim that unconditional love and unquestioned sense of security that I lost the last time I saw my mother.

The train stopped and we heard the sound of the bolts sliding across. The door was flung open. A blinding glare cut through the dimness of the carriage making us painfully aware of our dirt-encrusted clothing and rank odour. I blinked in the afternoon brightness. For one precious moment the soldiers, dogs, barbed wire fences and terrified faces of my family were obliterated. Then we were hurried off the train; men in striped uniforms hauled off those who could not manage on their own. Everyone crowded around the taps.

Somewhere a band was playing and instructions were being yelled over a microphone. In our innocence we were so grateful to be off the train. Days and days on board without food or water had perhaps clouded our judgement, we could only think of fresh air and water, water... that was what we craved most of all. At last we would be able to remove the dead, to stretch our legs, to drink.

We were dirty and tired and the end of the journey promised something to eat and somewhere to sleep. "You will be taken care of," promised the guards. "Just follow our orders."

I must have seen the barbed wire, the guard houses, the soldiers. I must have seen the strange look on the faces of those around me. I could not possibly have known what it all meant. I clung desperately to my mother's hand. Did I still believe that we were being taken to a labour camp? My father saw a Red Cross truck and was instantly relieved, "I'm going to see to your parents," he told my mother, "stay with the children."

I watched him walk towards the trucks with my grandparents and get swallowed up by the crowd. The elderly had suffered so much on the journey and were being promised much-needed medical attention. In the meantime on the ramp the guards were shouting orders and sorting us into groups. It seemed as though thousands and thousands of people were milling around in confusion and panic, shouting to each other, shouting for their children. My mother held on to my hand very tightly.

"Is this where we are going to live?" I asked my mother.

"Will Rachel and Leah be there? Why are these men so angry?"

"Hush," replied my mother, "we'll know everything soon."

"I don't like it here," Peiter said, starting to cry, "I want to go home. It smells bad!"

My mother hugged us close. She must have been as frightened as we were; she was certainly just as tired, hungry and thirsty. "Oh my boys, you are both so dirty, we will have to give you a bath as soon as possible!" There was comfort in the normality of her response to this abnormal situation.

Some tables had been set up to process the new arrivals. Attending the tables were doctors and soldiers. The sight of the doctors, like the Red Cross trucks, filled us with confidence. The Fatherland will look after us, in spite of us being Jews. The hardest part was over and the instructions given confirmed this belief. "You will be sorted into groups," explained the voice over the microphone. "From here you will be taken to the showers and given fresh clothes." We had all been demanding to know what was going on and complaining about the lack of facilities. The guards were shrugging off our complaints and questions, telling everyone not to worry, that it was now all over, and directing them towards several areas. When our turn came we were directed left but one of the soldiers came up to us and placed a rifle between my mother and me.

"You," he said motioning with his rifle, "you are going right."

"No!" stated my mother holding firmly onto my hand. "He is staying with me!"

She pulled me towards her. My mother was tall, but not as tall as the soldier, yet she raised her head and threw back her shoulders in defiance. No one was going to separate her from her son.

"Left!" yelled the soldier at my mother stepping in front of me.

"You go left, he goes right!"

"Mama! I want to stay with you!" I begged, as my hand slipped from her grasp.

"You cannot separate me from my children!"

She reached past him and grabbed hold of my hand again. And for the first time in that long nightmare of a journey, I watched as my mother lost all her composure. She began to scream, the words running into one another, colliding and falling over each other in their struggle to be heard: "This is inhuman. I will not go anywhere without him...We have suffered enough! Days and days in the heat locked into those dreadful carriages with no food or water, nowhere to sit, no facilities, not even able to get assistance for the elderly or the sick. What is the meaning of this, we are not animals! And now you want to take my son away from me? No! Enough! He comes with...!"

She never got to finish. The soldier had lost his patience. I saw a sudden movement and watched as my mother lost her grip on my hand and crumpled to the ground. It took me a few seconds to realise that the blood reddening her blouse was coming from the back of her head. I stared in horror and started to scream, grabbing hold of my mother as she struggled defiantly to her feet, her face white with anger and pain, oblivious to the danger, too new to camp sadism to understand the ramifications of her outburst. But others knew only too well. They knew that if this situation were not brought under control quickly the entire camp would suffer. They were the ones whose eyes had seen too much, they were the ones who knew the difference between right and left.

One of the doctors approached us. His face was drawn, he was thin. There was no pity left in his eyes. He addressed my mother calmly. "You will meet again inside. He will be safe, don't worry. You have to go that way now. He has to go this way."

He kept repeating over and over again "you have to go that way and he has to go this way but you will meet inside."

Finally my mother calmed down. She hugged me tightly, "Don't worry, we will be looking for you inside," she murmured. "Be brave, my son." And she turned and walked away.

That was the last time I was to see my mother and brother.

How could she know what she had been asking? How could she have known how futile her anger was? If she had known the true horror, what would have been her choice for her son, right or left? Could she have made that choice? What would have been my choice?

I stood alone on that ramp and watched my family walk away. I watched as the last familiar face was absorbed by the glare and vanished. I was surrounded by strangers. My stomach tightened in fear and panic as I began to search the crowd for someone I knew. Suddenly I was aware of being yelled at and turned just in time to deflect a blow to my head. I ran to join a group of strangers before another, better timed, blow sent me reeling. A lonely, frightened boy, not yet 10 years old, shaking and crying quietly. Why was this happening?

"I will see them inside, I will see them inside." Like a mantra, over and over again. "They will be waiting for me inside."

The tears dried. Something inside of me died then too. I had never seen violence before, never felt this hatred directed towards us before. I was in shock. For the first time, my mother had been unable to protect me, for the first time I was alone; all those from our village had already been processed or had been sent left with my mother.

Without understanding, tired and scared, I was motioned to a waiting group of men and boys. We were marched through the large imposing entrance, down an avenue of trees, past an impossibly green patch of lawn where the band had been performing, towards a large building. I clutched a card I had been given, the prize for being selected to go right, a prize that carried my new identity, that branded me not human enough to be known by name, only by a number. That card was my ticket into the hell of Auschwitz, a place that will forever be synonymous with evil.

The enormous, cavernous wooden building, with its wooden floors and high windows, was the quarantine barracks. More tables and more officers examined our cards and ordered us to strip. I was shy; I was too slow in removing my clothing. I kept looking around for someone, anyone, it didn't matter, just someone that I knew. The officer in charge didn't appreciate my restraint in removing my clothes and thought I needed some encouragement. Time seems to have passed by in a blur of beatings and loud voices. Naked, frightened and bewildered, I looked for my father among the men being shaved. Bruised and shaken, I had no more tears, there was nothing left to say, just the hope that they were waiting at the other end as promised.

I was grabbed, and my head shaved, too young to have hair anywhere else, at least I was spared that humiliation. A man grabbed my arm and within seconds had tattooed a number on the inside of my left arm - 111404. I stared at it in horror, Jews do not mark their bodies in this manner, it defiles the body, every child knew this, what were they doing, what did this number mean?

What does it mean to be reduced to a number? How can you know who you are when names no longer matter, when your mother is beaten in front of your eyes, and your father is no longer there; when you are stripped of every defining possession, every clue as to where you come from? We all looked the same: naked, bald, and frightened. Did it matter that the man standing next to me had, until recently, been the head of a large bank and was supposedly worth millions, or that the young boy ahead was considered a prodigy? We were now all the same, nameless, faceless creatures, the very lowest of the low. We survived the selection because we appeared able to work, or were useful in some way. It was just as well we did not know how we were to be used, for we would have gone mad in an instant, the mind cannot deal with too much information.

I did have an advantage, I was German, and so I understood the commands being yelled at us, unlike so many others who stared bewildered at the soldiers screaming orders at them in an incomprehensible language. But I understood and walked willingly into another area, a bath and disinfectant area. This I understood, my mother had trained me well, a bath would be good. But I was unprepared for the pain, how that water stung my skin, my freshly shaved head, my eyes. It seemed that each time I anticipated something based on my understanding of what should take place, the Nazis had a different, more painful and more dehumanising method. So by the time we were handed clothes, I was no longer expecting anything. Tired, confused, bruised from the regular prodding of batons, my skin and eyes stinging from the bath, I accepted the clothes I was given, clothes that certainly did not belong to me, but had been bought initially by a much larger man in another place and at another time, and then distributed, worn and disinfected many times over.

I peered closely at the men around me; none looked familiar, yet all looked the same. I no longer asked questions, I stopped looking for my father. Would I even recognise him in unfamiliar clothing without his beard, without any hair?

Four

I MET MIKHAIL AND ERHARDT ON THAT FIRST NIGHT. After I had been subjected to the unique Auschwitz initiation, tattooed, bare headed and stinging from a chemical shower, I was taken with a group of about 30 other men and boys on an interminable walk through a labyrinth of identical buildings that ended in a foul smelling, rat infested overcrowded barracks.

It was dark by the time I got to the barracks. The interior was lit by a dull electric lamp, the smell was overwhelming. In the gloom I made out a long narrow barn with wooden tiers on either side, and in the centre an aisle with a soft earth floor. Two small windows situated high up on the far wall reflected a bright red glow into the otherwise colourless interior. I shivered in the night air, more out of fear than cold for the air was thick with smells and sounds from many bodies.

Suddenly I heard an insistent whisper from above:

"Hey you, come up here, come up with us!"

Staring down at me from one of the upper tiers was a

dreadfully dirty, horribly skinny, fair-haired boy with the brightest blue eyes I had ever seen. His eyes grinned when I looked at him.

"Yes, you! Come on, climb up!"

I climbed up to the top tier and gagged. Cockroaches ran everywhere and the smell was worse at the top where it seemed to be intensified by the heat. The platform was so close to the ceiling that I had to roll onto it to lie down on the straw. My disgust was obvious for a second voice said rather ruefully, "Don't worry, you'll get used to it! I am Erhardt, this is Mikhail."

Erhardt was just as filthy as Mikhail and at this proximity I could see that both boys had caked excrement and blood on their tattered clothes and were covered in sores. Erhardt was older than Mikhail and myself by a few years, his dark hair had started to grow back indicating a while between disinfectant baths and there was a wisdom in his brown eyes that was well beyond his years.

"What is this place?" I asked, "and where are my parents? They will be looking for me, I need to find them."

Erhardt and Mikhail exchanged a quick look, and Erhardt replied quickly:

"We don't have much time to talk, but we have been here for six months already. If you want to survive you are going to have to be like us."

"We'll teach you what we do to stay alive here," added Mikhail, obviously proud of their ingenuity.

Alive! They looked barely alive themselves, covered in filth and sores, scratching at the lice that plagued them constantly, living in these squalid conditions, breathing in this putrid air. Is this living? They were both terribly thin; Erhardt's ears protruded so dramatically from the sides of his head that on any other occasion, Peiter and I would have really laughed. I wondered where Peiter was, where my family had been taken. Were they still looking out for me? In the distance, through the opening that served as a window, I could see a fire burning. Erhardt noticed me looking. "Try to get some sleep. They wake us very early for roll call; you need to get as much rest as you can. Don't worry, we'll look after you."

"But my parents..."

"Shh, we'll talk later, sleep now."

With the help of Erhardt and Mikhail I was taught that to survive meant only to live to see the next minute, the next hour. Every waking moment of life was a victory over death, over Mengele and his selections, over the Nazi regime that had decided to rid Europe of its entire Jewish population. Every morsel stolen or given meant death by starvation was kept at bay for that much longer. Every beating withstood meant that you had survived yet one more only to be vulnerable for the next. There were no survival tricks that caused one person to live and another to die.

Death was as random as the lottery and try as we might to find rational explanations for surviving a selection, for not being castrated, for being placed on a work detail that while being mundane and tedious was not overly taxing on our starving bodies, the only explanation I can come up with was that somehow, somewhere, the angels were watching over the three of us.

I wish I had known their family names or where they were born but that information had seemed irrelevant at the time. Entering Auschwitz, one was immediately stripped of one's identity and assigned a number. We all emerged looking the same, dressed in camp-issued clothing, with bald heads and vacant eyes. My number was important, that was who I was, names were a luxury we could ill-afford. Our childhood homes receded into the distance, the warmth and comfort we had known until then was irretrievable and far too painful to discuss, so we focused on the present and as a result the only knowledge I had of them was that they were also German. Our dehumanisation was so complete that even as children, and we were still children, we instinctively understood that from the moment we were pushed through the great gates of the camp, our lives had irrevocably changed. All that mattered was survival and the three of us were determined to survive.

Call it fate, good fortune or even destiny, but I had come across two boys whose support, kindness and caring were to carry me through my years at Auschwitz. They replaced the forty-four members of my family. They restored my faith in humanity in the face of abominable cruelty. We are not privy to the thoughts of God so we have no way of knowing His plan and can therefore never understand an event as horrific as the Holocaust, but I thank Him every day for giving me two such wonderful companions.

They taught me that while there was no place for children in Auschwitz, we could use our youth and the fact that we were German to our advantage. Essentially we were still children and so we drew from Auschwitz our own sense of meaning, accepted the cruelties, the murders, the selections, the never ending roll calls as part of a system we had to beat.

We knew that we were slave labourers, and expected to work like adults, that the moment we no longer had the strength to work would be the moment we died.

Having survived six months, Erhardt and Mikhail were both

well versed in the routines and workings of the camp and besides, there was a quiet confidence about Erhardt that immediately inspired my trust. So when he said, on that very first night that it was time to sleep, I knew my questions would be answered when the time was right and I obediently tried to find space on the platform.

There were about 10 people, men and boys, huddled on that one platform already, all vying for some personal space. Some settled down instantly - too tired, too hungry and too thirsty to do much else but escape into the tantalising world of dreams. Others tossed and turned, kicked, snored and shouted out. As soon as the lights were extinguished, to my horror I heard the scurrying of rats.

"Look at the size of that one!" Mikhail said suddenly. "Count them! Quick, see if you can count them!"

Kicks, curses, and yells reminding Mikhail that Auschwitz was not an amusement park for his personal enjoyment, however macabre, followed his outburst in rapid succession.

"He always does that," said Erhardt quietly. "It's one of his favourite games. It drives the others crazy but it keeps him going. Mikhail always manages to find some fun in everything, no matter how bad things are."

How could he find anything fun in this horrible place? I clung to the edge of the platform trying desperately to overcome the panic that was threatening to overwhelm me. Who were these people, why was I here, and above all, where were my parents?

The proximity of the 100 or so others in the barracks was disturbing. My mind was filled with images of my mother, hurt and bleeding, Peiter crying, old men and women being roughly handled and beaten, and above all, a sense of abandonment and bewilderment. I knew that I would soon resemble Erhardt and Mikhail: thin, gaunt and grey, covered with sores and filth. But what I didn't know was why. What had we done to be put here? What could all these people possibly have done to deserve this?

During that first night, I slept maybe one or two hours, disturbed every time someone moved, coughed or snored. Voices cried out in the dark - some in terror, some in joy, trapped in the false reality of their dreams. Every now and again someone's hand or foot broke through my façade of sleep, and as I turned, so too did the person lying next to me, and the person lying next to them, creating a domino effect, all the while the tiers creaking ominously. Everyone tried to avoid touching, as though the feel of another body was too intimate, too painful, too reminiscent of a time when touch meant love, not hatred; of a time when a touch was a caress or a hug, not a beating. I watched as men and boys recoiled from even the slightest physical contact, whether in sleep or awake. Touch meant pain.

The barracks themselves were hot, airless and overcrowded and we all fought for air and space. I learnt that they had once served as stables for the horses of the Polish army. I am sure the horses were more comfortable than we were.

Auschwitz was once just an ordinary town, with ordinary people. Its Polish name was Oswiecim. People came to visit: holidaymakers and tourists.

Today it still exists, only the tourists have changed. Those who come do so on a pilgrimage. They come to see the chimneys, to visualise the horror. They come to say *kaddish* over family members who disappeared without a trace, who were unceremoniously swallowed up by the raging fires. They come because it is a part of their past that they have to confront,

Jew and Gentile alike, for its very existence changed forever the possibility of Reason.

The world lost its innocence while the fires of Auschwitz burned and some go to mourn the loss of a time when answers appeared to be almost in reach.

Who can think of Auschwitz today without images of heaped corpses, walking skeletons, and chimneys belching fire and smoke? It carries its scars like all of us, transformed by experience, never to be the same again. On the shifting borders of Germany and Poland, Auschwitz was caught up in the Third Reich's quest for *Lebensraum*.

Like me, the town became a victim of Hitler's dream to restore the glory of the German people. Like me, the town became shrouded in lies and deceit, cleaned up, put on display, unbearably altered. But hidden beneath the surface is still the stink of burning corpses and rotting flesh. Dig just a little bit and unearth the horrors lying dormant, trapped within us both. Don't be fooled by the calm exterior, the remodelling, the bright and shiny surfaces, look closely and see the scars for they are there, they will always be there. I was a witness, I saw. I saw the chimneys belching smoke, saw the flames at night and smelt that undeniable smell that came from a building ironically referred to as 'the bakery'.

It took Erhardt a few days to be able to tell me about my parents. He put his arm around me after I had asked him a thousand times whether I would be seeing my family soon. He said very quietly: "All the smoke that you can see from the chimneys are all the people who come every day on the trains and go left instead of right.

"That's where your parents have gone, that's where mine have gone. We've just got to live ourselves, we have nobody.

I've got nobody, you've got nobody, Mikhail has nobody, we've just got to live ourselves."

He answered my unvoiced question."The chances of ever seeing your parents again? You won't. I've never seen mine again, Mikhail said he's never seen his parents again, so it's just us three."

For a boy to take on that awesome responsibility, for him to have to tell me what I had to know, that must have taken more courage than facing the SS soldiers. I stared at him, disbelieving...not wanting to believe. He kept his arm around me; it felt heavy on my shoulders, that first gesture of intimacy in days. Why did they leave me, why aren't they looking for me? How could my father let this happen? Didn't he love me enough? Wasn't I good enough or quick enough with my chores, hadn't I worked hard enough at school? I was hungry and thirsty and tired, I wanted my own bed in my own house amidst the vines. I wanted to run and hide in the forest with Rachel and Leah. I wanted some water so badly. Why had they left me here?

"Don't worry, we'll look after you," said Mikhail gently, "you're with us now."

I eventually had to acknowledge the truth of what I had been told. It was in the way Erhardt had spoken, the firm pressure of his arm and, of course, in what I saw every day. There was no room for doubt, however much I did not want to believe. I stared at the fires gleaming in the dark and resolved to do whatever I could to survive. I could take the abuse and the beatings; I could even cope with the lack of food. The three of us, we were invincible, we didn't need anybody else, certainly not adults. We would get out of here, we made plans, maybe we would go to America - the Golden Medina, because in

America we would be free. *Arbeit Macht Frei* - what a joke! Death for the inmates is the only freedom Camp Commandant Rudolf Höss has in mind. But if we succeed, if we survive, then the three of us will be truly free, we will call ourselves by name, we will forge a new path, a new identity, we will be pioneers and rise above the rest. Auschwitz will be our training ground; after all, as Mikhail kept saying, things can only get better!

Arbeit Macht Frei - Work Brings Freedom

FIVE

IN SEPTEMBER 1939 when The Third Reich began its occupation of Poland, the small town of Oswiecim in the Upper Silesia and its 12,000 occupants, 5,000 of whom were Jewish, came under German rule. The town was given the German name, Auschwitz. Today it still lies in the same humid and foggy valley created by two rivers, the Vistula and the Sola, near the snow-capped Tatra Mountains.

In the spring of 1940 a prison camp was created to house political prisoners, mainly Polish dissidents who resisted the occupation, with the aim of ridding the Reich of any opposition. SS-Hauptsturmführer (Captain) Rudolf Höss took command of the camp and began to transform the 16 single storey buildings that had served as the Polish army barracks into a concentration camp for those deemed undesirable by the Third Reich.

Three hundred Jewish residents of Oswiecim were brought in for six weeks to begin construction. In May that year, 30 German prisoners arrived, followed by 728 Polish inmates a month later, all from various criminal institutions. SS-Obersturmführer (First Lieutenant) Josef Kramer was appointed as Höss's deputy and Karl Fritsch was appointed chief of the prisoner camp.

All the residents from the surrounding areas were evicted to accommodate the growth of the camp and an empty area of 40 kilometres square was designated as belonging to the camp. The idea was to extend the camp to include workshops manned by prisoners for the manufacture of items that would assist in the German war effort. By March 1941, 10,900 prisoners were incarcerated in Auschwitz, most of them Polish. Then Himmler issued an order to increase the capacity of the camp to accommodate 30,000 prisoners and to establish at Brzezinka, a small town about three kilometres away, a camp large enough to hold 100,000 prisoners of war. This camp was named Birkenau. I.G. Farben, a large industrial company tempted by the prospect of access to cheap prison labour, expressed an interest in setting up operations in the vicinity of Auschwitz.

By the end of 1941, Auschwitz held as many as 18,000 prisoners and by 1943 it reached Himmler's goal of 30,000 prisoners living in an area 1,000 metres long and 400 metres wide. The camp also included living quarters for the SS, barracks for the SS guards, headquarters for the Auschwitz complex, a workshop and depot sector. The first section of the Birkenau camp was completed in 1942. By then Hitler had instigated his plan for the Final Solution, the projected annihilation of European Jews, and Birkenau was chosen as the major site for the mass exterminations.

Intensive expansion and the development of satellite camps saw some 40 different sections established over the wide area around Auschwitz, supplying the nearby mines, foundries and other industrial enterprises in the vicinity with a constant source of free labour. Most of the prisoners by this time were Jewish. Monowitz (Monowice) was the largest of these satellite camps and encompassed the I.G. Farben synthetic rubber plant (Buna Werke). They had hoped to profit from the available slave labour and expertise offered by the Jewish prisoners. Soon after my arrival in 1943, Höss was promoted for his efforts and replaced by SS-Oberstrumbannführer Arthur Liebenschel. The camp was divided into three distinct sections, Auschwitz I remained the main camp, Birkenau became known as Auschwitz II, and Monowitz and the surrounding smaller satellite camps became known as Auschwitz III.

Under the efficient leadership of Höss, Auschwitz had become the largest and most effective extermination centre in Europe. Through trial and error, Höss had discovered that the quickest and most reliable method of killing a large number of people without undue stress on the executioners was by gassing them, and the most efficient gas to use was Zyklon B, a poison used on rats and cockroaches. Disposal of the bodies was the next hurdle to overcome and here great ingenuity was shown. Once the bodies were stripped of anything and everything that could possibly be of use, including in some cases the skin, they were then transported to a crematorium for incineration. One crematorium became two, then three, and then four. The most efficient ways to burn the bodies were explored. It was discovered that a healthy strong body, meaning a new arrival to the camp, burned best when placed with an already emaciated prisoner, that is someone who had been in the camp a few months, and a child. Small children were often referred to as kindling because their young, soft bodies were so effective in fanning the flames within the crematoria. By the time I arrived in 1943, the process of killing and disposal was working very efficiently, the burning capacity of each crematoria reached 8,000 bodies on an average day.

The thing to remember is that those bodies were not just

nameless, faceless objects. Those bodies were our mothers, fathers, sisters, brothers. These bodies were once our children, our partners, our friends. They were artists, poets, philosophers, doctors, lawyers and farmers. They lived and breathed, laughed and cried. Some were good, honest and hardworking, some were not. They were my people, they were what gave my life its meaning, its rhythm, and they would have given my life colour and richness through their culture and language. Instead, their smoke blackened the air around Auschwitz, and their burning flesh smelled sickly-sweet against the stench of excrement and filth.

I was awoken suddenly, that first morning, by the sound of the barracks door being unlocked, followed by shouts and frantic activity. I had been aware of drifting in and out of consciousness rather than having had any real sleep and rather than feeling refreshed I awoke more exhausted. How can sleep itself be exhausting?

Erhardt was shaking me. "Hurry up," he said, "It's time for the latrines and roll call."

"I'm so tired," I groaned, "and I am really hungry and thirsty. Is it time for breakfast?"

"Yeah, we have a great breakfast waiting for us, just wait and see." Said Mikhail and then he laughed out loud, attracting the attention of one rather stern looking adult in prison stripes who cuffed him on the head with a gruff warning. Unperturbed, Mikhail grinned at me and winked.

Erhardt sighed, "He's going to get himself sent to the gas chambers one of these days."

"What gas chambers?" I asked.

Erhardt and Mikhail stared at me but did not answer my question. Instead they gave me a run down of how I was to behave during latrine time and roll call. Stand tall. Be quick when you go to the toilet. Don't be late for roll call. This is a very strange place. You must learn the rules. Do not attract attention to yourself. If you want to know anything, ask us, no one else. You can't trust anybody here, least of all the adults.

I felt my world crumbling around me. Adults, warm, loving and kind had always surrounded me. They had fed me, clothed me, taught me and given me a sense of security. I had always trusted adults. They held authority and knew what was best. Why were these different?

"They will steal from you and beat you," said Mikhail matter-of-factly. "They all do that. They are mad here - you'll soon find out."

We moved out of the barracks towards the latrines. The sky was velvet in the predawn darkness. Bright searchlights erected on high fences mocked the moon with their harsh brilliance. I saw row upon row of large barns for further than my eye could see. There were no signs of life anywhere: I had come to a place where only the dead walk free. Strange, hollowed-eyed men jostled past without seeing me. I felt like a shadow, insubstantial, ephemeral and light-headed, the scene before me unfolding with a nightmarish sense of unreality.

The path was soft and slimy beneath my feet. There was no evidence of the green trees and lawns I had noticed at the entrance. The shoes I had been issued were large and ill-fitting and allowed the marshy earth to seep in between my toes.

Mikhail, irrepressible even at this early hour, saw my discomfort. "It will be OK," he said in a whisper. He put his arm across my shoulders, "Erhardt will take care of you, just like he takes care of me."

"I want to go home." I said in a small voice. "I want my

mother and father and my brother and my grandparents to be there. I want the forest and the vines. I don't like this place it scares me."

Mikhail gave my shoulder a squeeze: "We are stuck here. There is nowhere else to go."

We arrived at the toilet block and to say the latrines were a shock would be a gross understatement. Mikhail grinned when he saw the revulsion on my face. "You will get used to it. Some of the adults never do, but you will. Look at that old man, he is constantly trying to wash himself but there is so little water that he never really manages, but I guess it makes him feel better. And that guy, look at him...he has his shirt and his cap clasped between his knees in case someone steals them, and they will too, you know. Hey, we would steal them! We are much quicker than these old men. They don't stand a chance against us. Don't use the soap, they say it is made from dead bodies and it really stinks, anyway. We would rather not wash at all."

Mikhail kept up a steady stream of chatter throughout what constituted the morning ablution. I was to learn that there were very few situations in which Mikhail did not keep up a steady stream of chatter. He was indefatigable, no matter how parched his throat or empty his belly, he never ran out of things to say, nor did he lose his spirit. Erhardt, on the other hand, remained quiet and watchful. He noticed everything, occasionally pointing out various opportunities or problems, or drawing our attention to the erratic behaviour of the other inmates.

Just as we were leaving the latrines Erhardt pulled me aside sharply, "Here, quick. Don't say a word, just take a sip."

The latrines were housed in a large wooden barn and wedged between two planks just under the eaves was a small tin containing a splash of murky liquid. It had been cleverly concealed both for safety and to prevent evaporation during the day. I quickly took a sip and gagged. The water was bitter and tasted of metal but it was sufficient to cool my burning throat. Erhardt grabbed the tin and returned it to its hiding place. The entire process had taken about 10 seconds. I was impressed. The tin was no longer visible to the eye. As we walked towards the roll-call area, Erhardt explained that the water had been collected during the last rainfall and had been sitting there for a while but was still okay. It was usually used for emergencies only, however as I had yet had nothing to eat or drink, he had felt justified in sharing this very precious resource.

I was confused, how could water be a precious resource? I had seen taps in abundance on our arrival. I remembered how my mother and the other passengers had run to them to fill up whatever containers they could. We had all drunk freely. Also, I knew we were close to a river because the soil in the camp was marshy. There should be no shortage of water in this region. I mentioned this. Erhardt looked at me in exasperation but said quietly, "Don't look for things to make sense here, they don't. And anyway if you think you have found an answer, you will find that the rules change the next day. We have to take care of ourselves here. You will have to learn how to take whatever advantage you can, whenever you can. You never know when you might need something and everything has a value. Even those odd shoes of yours!"

I looked down at my feet, thinking who would possibly want

this broken mismatched pair of shoes, when all of a sudden the air crackled with tension.

"It's the Kapos!" whispered Mikhail. "Here we go again!"

"Both of you, stand up straight and don't say a word. If they hit you, just bite your lip, say nothing!" muttered Erhardt urgently under his breath.

"Why would they hit me?"

"Shut up!" growled Erhardt in reply.

"But I haven't done..."

The baton caught me on the side of my head and sent me reeling. I felt hot tears pricking my eyes and could taste blood in my mouth. I had bruised my knees in my fall and my head was spinning. Overhead I could hear the voice of the kapo screaming at me as if from a far distance. Incomprehensible words washed over me, I understood the language but the words made no sense. Why was he so angry, what had I done wrong? Why was I being punished?

Six

"STAND UP, IF YOU DON'T THEY WILL KILL YOU."

Erhardt's whispered words cut through the confusion and pain like a hot knife through butter. I pulled myself up. The kapo glared at me and I was too afraid to move.

My first experience of roll call left me exhausted from standing still for hours on end. My new friends stood a bit closer so that I could lean on them, then abruptly I would stand straight again as a guard approached. I bit my lip to stop the tears falling and concentrated on trying to remain upright.

Many days passed before I understood the enormous amount of strength it took for Mikhail and Erhardt to support me for those long hours. Although I had lost some weight on the journey into Auschwitz, I still weighed more than either boy who, after being in the camp for six months, were beginning to resemble the victims of a devastating famine.

The pain in my head was enough of a reminder to keep quiet and so we stood in silence, the three of us, or rather they stood and I leaned, for another three hours while the moon slowly faded under the onslaught of the early morning summer sun. We stayed there on that marshy parade ground as the humidity settled around us with the steam and heat rising up from the very ground on which we stood.

Time moves very slowly. Every now and again we stood to attention while someone tried to count us.

"Tallest in the front, children at the back!"

And the shuffle began while all the time the kapos hit out with whips and batons at anyone who did not appear to be moving quite fast enough.

Then again, after a while, "No, that is not right, do the shorter ones in front this time and count again."

And again, and again.

And all the while the sun climbed higher and higher and the smell got worse and worse. Images twisted in front of my eyes, floated past my vision, my eyelids kept wanting to shut them out and my feet felt as though they had long since left the ground. I saw men, tall, immaculately dressed men, with rifles and batons. I saw them beat an old man in front of me mercilessly for no apparent reason. I watched that man, as if in a dream, screaming and begging for mercy. I watched as he stopped crying out and yet the soldiers continued to kick him until finally, after what seems like an eternity, I watched them toss his lifeless body to the side of the parade ground. I stood there shaking uncontrollably. I felt as though I was on fire with no escape from the flames. My throat was parched, like kindling it breathed new life into the fire; my skin was burned and instinctively recoiled from the heat of the relentless summer sun. I felt dry, brittle, ready to crack.

I stared past the impassive soldiers down the rows of barracks towards the double electrified fences and the guard towers that surround the camp. Past the fences, the green fertile fields and forests of the region taunted us. Beyond that, the people of the surrounding towns and villages went on with their ordinary lives, making the necessary adjustments to accommodate German rule. They still woke in their own beds, surrounded by their families and got on with the day to day tasks of living. I had given up any hope of seeing my family again, these monsters have stolen them from me, and with them, my soul.

If civilisation is the veneer that hides the animal within us then Auschwitz stripped that veneer not only from its inmates but also from its guards and with it went every last vestige of humanity, and the baseness of the human condition was exposed to the world. The survival instinct, so strong in animals, resurfaced, annihilating the moral and ethical principles that control every person throughout his or her life. No longer were even the ten simple rules handed down to Moses on Mount Sinai, relevant. In this nightmarish world we would kill, covet, steal and commit adultery. We would forsake our God in the belief that He had forsaken us. We would worship the idols that we created to make sense of our world. For, like whipped puppies panting at the heels of a cruel master, we would follow the German guards to our deaths, obedient and docile, in the hope that it would bring us one more piece of bread, buy us one more day and maybe bring us one step closer to redemption.

On that first dawn, stripped of my past and everything that I had known and loved, I was forged by the heat of the sun into an Auschwitz animal: sly, cunning and deceitful. Erhardt was the blacksmith who fashioned the tool, Mikhail his assistant. Together, the three of us were changed forever, each by the other and the circumstances in which we found ourselves. We found strength in the other, we learned that the whole is so much more than merely a sum of its parts, and we determined to try to remain together wherever possible.

As it turned out, we were fortunate for, as much as we willed it, our fate did not rest in our hands. Perhaps in some bizarre way the angels were looking out for us. It is the only explanation that I can find; our angels must have been working overtime on that day because when we were finally allowed to leave the parade ground we were each assigned a work detail and much to our delight we were sent to the same workshop. And so my life in Auschwitz began.

Every day was the same, business as usual. No matter what happened, what the weather was like, how weak you felt, whether there was food or not, it was business as usual. Our day began at three a.m. The bolts of the barracks would open noisily and the shouting and beating would begin. We would go to the latrines, and then assemble for roll call on a dark parade ground. Sometimes it would be icy cold and we would stand there shivering in the pre-dawn air, occasionally moving about according to the whim of the Kapo on duty. Too early for the SS guards, we would stand for hours waiting for them. Our feet would ache, our legs would feel like lead but still we stood. If someone had died in the night or while on roll call, we would have to hold up the dead body to be counted. Sometimes this went on for days until a death cart came by and removed the body. Then, and only then, could the body be ticked off the register.

With the passing of every day I could feel weakness and lethargy invade my body. Merely climbing off the bunk became a supreme effort of will. My mind was dulled by hunger, my body sore from beatings, my throat burned with thirst. There seemed to be no way to avoid upsetting the guards. If you were too slow. they would beat you, if you moved too quickly, they would beat you, if you stood still, they would beat you. If you caught their eye, they would beat you, if you didn't look at them, they would beat you. They were so methodical but their methods were so unusual you never knew what they were going to do.

And so we cowered and slithered, behaving more and more like the vermin they told us we were. But like vermin, we learnt survival strategies and quickly adapted to the ever-changing conditions imposed upon us. Perhaps, as children, we accepted our fate far easier than the men around us. The faces of our past vanished in the putrid air, taking with them the memory of the warmth and love of our mothers, the comfort of home and the security we had once known. I was 111404, I was a pig, a rat, a piece of shit. I was merely another thing to be used and abused by anyone who was so inclined, with the exception of Mikhail and Erhardt. Together we were once again human, once again important: we called each other by name. Together we could laugh, but we could not and would not cry, not then, not for a very, very long time.

Together, we were assigned work in a metal plate workshop in Monowitz. Our task was to stack the plates after they had been pressed. It was mind-numbingly tedious work but it was better than the senseless labour imposed by the SS on many of the inmates. In the workshop we were relatively safe. To be safe in Auschwitz meant to be indoors, not to be worked to death and so we were safe, protected, we were among the lucky ones.

We couldn't talk much while we worked as the guards constantly patrolled the workshop beating and prodding the prisoners, urging them to work faster and faster, or sometimes just having a bit of fun by tormenting some poor defenceless *musselman*. I never found out where that term came from, but I understood its meaning from the start. Children are so black and white and everything is taken so literally. It did not take me long to absorb that word into my understanding of Auschwitz. *Musselman*: a prisoner whose body is completely wasted by hard work, hunger and disease. His leathery skin is drawn taut across his bones exposing his vulnerability, his eyes were fixed to the ground as though the mere effort of raising his gaze required too much strength. His back is bent and his arms hang lethargically by his sides. His movements are incredibly, painfully slow. We were determined never to become *musselman*, we hated them more than we hated the German soldiers who beat us, we also feared them more. They represented our future, those pitiful bags of bones were what we would end up like, and so we avoided them at all costs and treated them with scorn and disdain.

We had been raised in an environment where most decisions were left to adults we trusted. As children we did not have to worry about basic necessities, we took them for granted. This was our life and we did not question it. How innocent and accepting we once were! They had always made the rules and never before had we cause to question their judgement or decisions. And now we found ourselves in a situation ruled by adults who were cruel, heartless men and women in smart, clean uniforms, with batons and whips. But we obeyed because we had to and because that was all we knew. Memories of tenderness, of warmth, of the feeling of a full belly did not vanish overnight but were rather nudged, ever so slowly, into the recesses of our memories, escaping occasionally in dreams making waking to the Auschwitz reality even harder. This nightmare of shouted orders, strict routines, minimal food, and beatings became our world and we accepted it. We didn't understand it, but we accepted it anyway and we learnt the routines well, played the system as it was, allowing us to survive just that little bit longer.

"Don't trust them," Erhardt would say over and over again to Mikhail and I, referring not only to the guards but to the other adults imprisoned with us as well. "If you want to know anything, ask me. I will tell you the truth. Don't ask them for anything either and don't tell them if you have any extra food or anything else. They will kill you, beat you or steal from you." He was so confident, so sure of himself, even the guards seemed to notice it for he certainly did not get beaten as frequently as everyone else did. I also noticed how the other children around would flock to Erhardt for help in a dispute or just for a few words of comfort. I wondered why he had chosen me.

SEVEN

THE FIRST THING ERHARDT PROCURED FOR ME was a piece of string to hold up my pants. It wasn't a very long piece, it was just a regular piece of twine, the kind we used every day on the farm. I remember my father's large capable hands sitting of an evening playing with such a piece of string, or during the day, tying the vines to the stakes so that they grew strong and straight. It was just an ordinary piece of string in any world other than Auschwitz for in Auschwitz that piece of string had a value far beyond what a piece of string should ever have.

I had been issued with some clothes upon arrival but the pants had obviously once belonged to a far bigger man. I had managed to roll up the leg so that I could walk without tripping but no matter how far down I rolled the waistband, my pants insisted on slipping down. This had caused me endless problems during roll call where we were required to stand as still as possible. Of course if any of the kapos or the soldiers happened to notice that my pants were falling down, I would be lucky to get away with a cuff to the side of my head from a baton or a fist in my face as punishment. The fact that these pants had been issued by the very same people who were now berating the fact that they were falling down and punishing me for it was beyond my comprehension.

How does a child understand such logic? He doesn't. I accepted the blame for my falling pants and for shuffling in line; I accepted the fact that I was a stupid fool, a Jewish pig, unable to even keep his pants up. I believed what they told me, and so did Mikhail and most others, but Erhardt took it upon himself to organise a piece of string for me to tie up my pants. He had noticed me trying to keep them up by knotting and folding the waistband without much success and realised that I was attracting some unwelcome attention. He understood the consequences of that with much greater clarity than I did.

We had gathered at the latrines, the one time we had some freedom to talk. The latrines were busy; there were people from all different barracks meeting and exchanging information. I could hear many different languages being spoken; I sensed the distrust among the different nations. This was by no means a homogenous group of people.

Erhardt slid the rolled up twine into my palm and closed my fingers around it. Even then I understood its value and was amazed at his ability to find me something so rare. He told me about the bartering system he had been using for some months and I thanked him. What had he traded, I wondered, to find this precious gift for me? Mikhail gave me a smile. He was so trusting, so open. I wondered many times how he kept his faith and his humour. I believe that Erhardt had a lot to do with it. Under his protection and tutelage, we both thought we were invincible. Without Erhardt to guide us, I don't believe Mikhail and I would have survived for very long.

Erhardt made it possible for us to find meaning in whatever we did. He was extraordinarily brave; taking anything the German SS would throw at him with dignity and they in turn seemed to develop a respect for him for they left him alone probably because he was very good at controlling the other children in the barracks. I was so proud to be by his side. I had no idea what that piece of string cost him, a piece of bread perhaps, black and stale, cherished because it was the only thing standing between survival and starvation. Or perhaps an errand run. Erhardt was secretive, often coming and going quietly without any explanation. If we asked where he had been, he would just answer that he was taking care of things. And we benefited from his expeditions, Mikhail and I, sometimes we would get a half-eaten piece of bread, other times something much needed like my piece of string. With the string around my pants, I felt like a millionaire.

The following morning Erhardt told me it was time for me to meet the British airmen working in the shed. Instantly I was afraid. I did not want to meet anyone. How did he know we can trust them. He has told me to trust no-one, so why them?

He told me they are Prisoners of War and officers, so they occasionally get Red Cross parcels. I could not concele my amazement when he said they once gave him a piece of chocolate. Chocolate! Real chocolate in Auschwitz? Impossible! I had not tasted chocolate for so long. Children should always be easily swayed by the possibility of something sweet and delicious to eat. And yet Auschwitz had tempered even that instinct and I was wary. It sounded too good to be true. I did not want to have to rely on any adults ever again. I was no longer expecting kindness or concern from the adults around us. Even the adults in our barracks who, under any other circumstances would have been our protectors, our teachers and our leaders, were now our enemies, fighting with us over the last bowl of soup, stealing whatever they could from us, using our youth and inexperience to their advantage. I had good reason to be suspicious of an adult offering chocolate.

He tried to quell my concern by telling me they sometimes pass on information about what is going on in the camp. The SS have to be careful how they treat Prisoners of War because the Red Cross keeps in touch with them, he explains. He saw that I was still apprehensive so to clinch the deal he added that there was a chance of chocolate for me too, then he gave me what would prove to be a rare grin, never knowing that it was his smile that won me over, not the chocolate.

The British Airmen certainly looked a lot better fed than us, but then that is not very difficult under the circumstances. I had met them on my first day in the workshop where they worked the huge machine that pressed the metal into plates. It was very hard for us to communicate and in any event we did not really have much of a chance because of the continual presence of the SS. Talking on the job was a terrific excuse for a good beating and I was to discover that although there was no real need for our guards to find an excuse, they did like to feel justified. In spite of this, Erhardt and one of the airmen named Norman still managed to exchange a few words and we got to know one another pretty well over the next couple of years.

I became accustomed to the rhythm of Auschwitz. Even hell has its own beat. Being so young and used to the rigour of farm life, I adjusted quickly. My body became used to operating on limited resources. Sometimes everything seemed ephemeral, as though the wire fences could just melt away and the whole camp seemed to be on the verge of dissolving into the thick, moist air. Sometimes I felt as though I was merely floating through it all, lacking substance. Even the beatings on those days did not seem real. Then there were other days when I could barely crawl out of bed, feeling thick and heavy, and every movement was an extreme effort of will. On those days, the blows seemed harder, the guards crueller. Yet the rhythm of the camp never changed: sleep, work, sleep, work.....

Eventually even my sleep patterns began to accommodate the patterns of those others crammed with me on the bunk. I fell asleep listening to the snores and groans of the sleepers around me, hugging the very end of the bunk and waking up in pretty much the same position, clutching onto the end as if onto a life raft.

I slept and woke under the red glow from the chimneys at Birkenau. A tiny window at the barracks framed the square chimneys. A constant reminder of what would happen to us if we did not behave.

We accepted death the way some kids accept an inevitable punishment – philosophically. Every day we faced death, every day we saw death. There is no mystery surrounding death, it is ugly and violent. In the camp it wore immaculate uniforms and hid behind beautiful faces but we knew who it really was, it had taken our families and was waiting to take us. We feared the beatings more than death; it is harder to live than to die in Auschwitz. And when our time comes we know we are not going to beg or plead, we are going to shout

out our names proudly as we pass in the truck heading for the ovens, just as those boys did, the ones who had not made the selection that week. I will shout: "I am Bernard Holstein, son of Jurgen and Magda, grandson of Jochim and Miriam Weissmantel! I lived here and I will die here. Do not forget me or what the Germans are doing to us." I will shout this proudly if given the chance. Maybe someone will one day meet my father, or an uncle or an aunt, who perhaps would remember a little boy called *Benoni* by his mother who was sent to Auschwitz. They will say that I met death bravely, that I remembered my name; that I remembered my family; that even in that moment of death I knew who I was and where I had come from. And that knowledge...that knowledge is our greatest defiance, the most effective resistance to the Nazi plan to exterminate the Jewish People because we remember and ensure that we are remembered. We will keep the memory of our parents and grandparents, aunts, uncles and cousins alive and through us, they too will survive, they will survive through our stories, as Jews have survived for 5,000 years through the stories of the Torah. We will survive and tell of those who did not, so that they too will not be forgotten.

Eight

UNDER THE PROTECTION OF ERHARDT I survived my first few weeks in the camp. Erhardt and Mikhail had survived six months already. They knew what we had to do. I listened to Erhardt. He had told me that if I didn't, I wouldn't last the month.

He taught me some basic rules: Don't make eye-contact with any of the guards; and keep everything you own on you at all times, especially your shoes and any morsels of bread.

Around me people are dying daily by the thousands. They work them to death here, all they feed us is disgusting soup, something hot they call coffee, and some black bread. There is never anything fresh to eat and very little water. We are constantly hungry and thirsty.

Mikhail read my thoughts and to comfort me he explained that it is just until this war is over, but Erhardt was quick to remove his rose-coloured glasses and impatiently told him he is too trusting. He was right and I vowed not to make that mistake.

Erhardt proved to be a valuable teacher and so when he said one morning that I was to volunteer for an assignment, I unhesitatingly raised my hand alongside his and Mikhail's without needing any knowledge of what that assignment would be.

About 20 boys around our age were chosen. I began to get nervous when we were separated from the rest of the group. I had been separated from a group before and I never saw any of them again. I sought reassurance from Erhardt, but once again it was Mikhail who made me feel better by grinning and winking at me.

"Mikhail!" said Erhardt very sternly, "Calm down! Now don't muck up this time, just listen to me and do what I say. Remember what happened last time, we were lucky. They'll be watching this time more carefully."

"I'll be more careful, I promise," said Mikhail absent-mindedly picking at a sore on his arm. "It's just that I get so hungry when I see all that food."

"Food! What food?"

"That's where we're going today," grinned Mikhail. "Our assignment is to clean the officers' mess. Usually we go there about three times a week, but with all the new...."

"Sshhhhhh!"

The soldiers had finished whatever it was that they were doing with the rest of the group and had returned to focus attention on us. Orders were being yelled amidst curses and blows and within seconds we were lined up in rows of three and marched off down the muddy roads between the barracks towards the large imposing building that stood alongside the kitchen.

The minute I walked into the officers' mess I was assailed by the memory of my mother. I could feel her in the air, in the smell of sausage and cabbage that hangs around the room, a reminder of things lost. I was poked in the back by Erhardt and brought back to the present. The soldiers were issuing instructions and Erhardt was making sure that I was listening.

Do not to try and eat any of the leftover food; they know what scavengers we are and will be checking on us at all times.

The leftovers are to be thrown into the bins outside.

All crockery and cutlery will have to be accounted for before we leave for they know what thieving trash we are.

Anyone caught taking food out of the mess or eating anything will be punished. They know what was left and we are not to think that we can get away with anything.

I, of course, believed them. Why wouldn't I? I was nine years old, although tall enough to pass for twelve; I have not the guile of a twelve-year-old. Fortunately Erhardt does.

"There's no way that they know what is on the plates," he whispered. "They are just bluffing. But you do have to be careful. Don't take everything, empty plates make them suspicious. Just a little at a time. And don't try and hide anything on you, especially anything that will leave a mark, like something oily or wet. They search us when we leave. Last time Mikhail walked out with a piece of bread. I was so angry with him. They kill you for that here. He was lucky though and got away with it."

The tables had to be cleared, the plates stacked and taken to the kitchen for washing. All the leftover food had to be thrown into the outside bins where contented rats the size of small kittens played happily. We were searched when we left the building and when we returned. The soldiers laughed at us and mocked us, teasing us with talk of their meal and how delicious the sausage or the strudel had been. They call us Auschwitz Rats, fighting over discarded food and then beat us when they caught us with the core of an apple or a discarded piece of cake.

Mikhail was adept at handling beatings. Irrepressible even under the worst of conditions, he is forever doing something wrong, and so out of the three of us he is the one who most often caught a beating. Sometimes he would allow himself to be propelled by the blow rather than resist it and in this way reduce its impact. As long as he got back on his feet quickly, he usually managed to look suitably mortified so as not to attract any more beatings. And yet in all that time, I never once saw him cry, not even after the worst of beatings. In Auschwitz you could not spare the fluid needed for tears.

It was not that the German soldiers reacted to Mikhail with any kind of compassion, rather they gave him the same consideration one would a disobedient animal. Dirty, scrounging for food, covered with sores and lice, we were not a loveable bunch of kids by any stretch of the imagination and as far as the Germans were concerned we were so far removed from their own children as to not even be of the same species. We were nothing more than pests. Their assignment to the camps was a double-edged sword because although it kept them from confronting any real danger, it also kept them bored. Like the bullies they were, they took out their frustrations on those weaker than themselves, on the half-starved children, those godforsaken innocents born under the Star of David.

And we accepted it, the brutality, the lack of food, the harsh conditions, and we learned what it takes to survive. And we were lucky. We were lucky to have escaped the initial selection on the ramp, we were lucky not to get a beating from a particularly vicious guard, we were lucky to be able to clean the mess a few times a week and scrounge a few crumbs off each plate and so postpone death by starvation for that much longer, and we were lucky we worked indoors doing easy labour. We were lucky, extremely lucky.

And our luck held out, at least for a while, for under the direction of Erhardt we learned to take only a little off each plate while no one was looking. As it turned out, often the guards had eaten very well and had drunk very well too and so were quite often rather dull and lethargic, particularly in the summer when the sun lingered in the sky and the workday was long. Then they would laze around outside, smoking a precious cigarette or finishing off a glass of schnapps, occasionally giving one of the boys a hard time just for the fun of it but without any real malice. Bellies full and light-headed from too much illicit alcohol, they were no match for the quick wit and cunning of Erhardt. He showed us that if you hid food inside the roll of your pants or in the turned up sleeve of your jacket it was undetectable even when searched. He taught us to eat without seeming to by taking only small bits of food that can be swallowed quickly. We saw what happens when you get caught with food in your mouth.

He was a young boy, starving like the rest of us, but careless. He had walked outside towards the bins when a guard stopped him.

"Hey you! What have you got in your mouth?" bellowed the guard.

"Nothing." The boy gave the only response he could under the circumstances while at the same time trying to push the food he could not swallow under his cheeks.

"Open your mouth."

He opened his mouth and the guard saw nothing, just rotting teeth and bleeding gums. The guard, not to be outdone with all his mates watching, took the boy's face in his large hand intending only to scare him but in doing so squeezed his cheeks. Out oozed what was once strudel. This was a bad situation because the guard could not back down in front of his friends, even if he had wanted to, and so the boy had to be punished. Angry with himself for being painted into a corner, the guard gave that boy a particularly vicious beating. We heard the sounds of laughter from the watching guards, the thud of the small body hitting the ground, the snap of bone against boot.

Erhardt had looked pointedly at Mikhail as if to say: "You see what can happen?"

I just stared in mind-numbing horror, and resolved to always obey Erhardt.

We had to carry the boy back to the barracks because he could no longer walk. Barely conscious, each movement was agony and yet he only moaned occasionally. He died sometime during the night. In the morning we had to bring his body out so that he could be ticked off the roll. We stood holding his dead body for five hours, shuffling backwards and forwards, while the day got hotter and hotter and the body heavier and heavier. Such a small body, beaten to death for having a morsel of food in his mouth that no one else wanted. Such was the logic of Auschwitz. Here we were, half-starved while the officers feasted to excess, sent to clean up after them and not even allowed to eat what they had discarded and then being blamed for our hunger as though somehow it was all our own doing.

NINE

MY GOD, WE WERE HAPPY that night after the Mess! With our bellies a little fuller we felt we could conquer the world. We went through the now familiar evening rituals with enthusiasm. I even managed to hide a bit of black bread. I was learning fast that any advantage was worth capitalising on. That bit of bread was camp currency, the more currency one had, the more power one had. We felt like children again. I remember laughing at Mikhail's stupid jokes, I even remember Erhardt smiling and relaxing just a little. We clamoured onto the top bunk laughing at our good fortune.

"How often do we get to do this?" I ask Erhardt.

"Oh, maybe three or four times a week," he replied. "Is it not great? Only be careful," he drops his voice to a low whisper, "the others get very jealous. They know we get extra food and they try to steal it from us or bully it out of us so stay alert."

Suddenly Mikhail crouched on all fours on the bunk and jumped. The distance between the bunks is about 10 feet. According to Erhardt, Mikhail had been trying to make a clean jump across to land squarely on the opposite bunk for months but has so far failed miserably each time, much to the annoyance of the surrounding occupants. This time was no exception. Erhardt and I shrieked with laughter.

"Stupid idiot! Get off me!" yelled a man who happened to be standing in the very spot Mikhail landed.

"What are you trying to do? Do you want the bunks to come falling down?"

"What do you think this is, the circus?"

"The boy is an idiot! He'll bring the kapo in here in a minute!"

Ignoring the complaints, Mikhail scrambled back up to our bunk. "Next time I'll do it," he said grinning, "I was really close this time!"

"Mikhail, you have to be careful. These bunks are so rickety, any extra weight and they will collapse, you know that," said Erhardt with an exasperation he doesn't really feel. It was so good to laugh again, to feel young again; I wanted to hold on to that moment. I was nine years old and I suddenly felt very, very old.

Everyone knew what has happened to The boy who had been beaten, or rather those who cared knew. And people cared for different reasons. Some cared because the boy had a jacket, cap, spoon or cup that is now available; others cared because his spot on the bunk was a better one than theirs. We were just grateful it was him and not us for we knew it was only luck that allowed us to steal food without getting caught; luck and Erhardt's cunning. Our exhilaration was a reaction to the risk we had taken. The greater the risk, the greater the satisfaction. We had risked our lives for a bit of extra food; it had to mean everything. That boy was an example of what could happen. So were the two boys hanging on the gallows at the entrance to our camp.

What possible infraction could these starving boys have committed to justify the horror of death by hanging? And yet there they hung, two of them, their bodies not yet hardened by adolescence, swaying gently in the fetid air. An example of what could and would happen if we did not obey the rules. The gallows stood at the end of the camp, behind them the double electric wire fences strung between the sentry boxes. Trees loomed like sentinels beyond the camp fence. A few kilometres away the tall chimneys belched black smoke into the air. Reminders of the many ways to die in Auschwitz.

The long days of summer were gradually coming to an end and although we were grateful at the time for the relief from the humidity and the heat, Erhardt began to worry about how we were going to survive the winter. He and Mikhail had already experienced the horror of an Auschwitz winter with inadequate food and clothing. I was still blissfully unaware how painful it could be to stand on a hard icy ground with freezing swollen feet in temperatures well below zero for hours on end. Erhardt knew that we would have to find some shoes and some warmer clothing. As always he was one step ahead of us.

One morning while we were standing on the parade ground I felt a chill in the air and breathed in the familiar snow smell that comes off the northern mountains. It is the same smell that I knew from home, a smell that signalled the start of long conversations around a hot stove in a warm kitchen, and thick woollen sweaters and scarves knitted by my mother and grandmother. It is a smell that meant *Rosh Hashanah* was close, *Yom Kippur* and *Succoth*. It meant that my mother and grandmother would have been baking sweet things for the New Year, honey cakes and *taiglach*, while my father would come in smelling sweet of the grapes he had been harvesting for pressing.

Now it meant a renewed battle for survival because the rules of the Auschwitz survival game changed in winter. Almost overnight the cracked window, priceless in summer, now posed an alarming threat. What was once a welcome breath of fresh air offering some relief from the stifling heat, now threatened to freeze us during the night.

It is hard to sleep when you are cold and the wind seemed to single me out for special attention. I broke a cardinal Auschwitz rule and tried to move closer to Erhardt hoping to share some body heat, but he elbowed me away, defensive even in sleep.

"Are you cold?' whispered Mikhail.

I nod.

"Me, too. I don't mind if you lie closer to me. That way we might both manage to get warm."

We lay close together, like the children we no longer were.

The following day we did not go to the workshop. About 20 of us were chosen and taken from the roll call area in the morning.

"Where are we going?" I ask.

"Shh, I know what you know," whispers Erhardt worriedly.

We had reason to worry; changes in routine were not usually a positive thing. Boys had been taken from roll call and never seen again, some had come back forever changed, as though something unseen had been irrevocably altered and others had come back just the same as before. You just never knew.

This time we were lucky. Two guards escorted us to a courtyard near the kitchen. In the courtyard was a large shed and piled around were bags and bags of potatoes and some empty drums. We were issued with peeling knives.

"Fill the drums with peeled potatoes!" barks one of the guards.

We found some empty drums to sit on, and positioned ourselves around the bags of potatoes and drums that we had to fill and started peeling.

"These potatoes are rotten," whispered Mikhail, "Look they fall through your fingers."

"Shut up, pig!" yelled the guards, "Start peeling!"

Erhardt waited until the guards had settled down and then whispered to us: "Just cut the ends of the good potatoes off and hide them in your mouth and chew them when you can. Don't get caught!"

We all did as he said. We pushed the chewed potato up into the sides of our mouths between our gums and cheek. By poking our tongues into the chewed potato we can get some of the juice. Then we swallowed and started again.

Several hours later our drums were full and we are returned to the barracks without incident. We knew we were lucky on this occasion but there were other occasions when we were not so lucky and returned to the barracks beaten and blue with cold. Nonetheless, that little bit of extra food, even if it was a raw potato, meant that we were that much further from starvation, that much more resilient to the hundreds of viruses and bacteria that seemed to ravage the camps unchecked. We had only our lives to lose and they, as our guards were constantly reminding us, were not worth that much in any event. Our youth made us brave and we took risks. We were impatient with the adults, not understanding that they had so much more to lose. They had wives and children somewhere, maybe even in the camp, a business or a profession to return to one day. They had invested years building themselves up to be someone and something; they had worked hard, educated themselves, and achieved in their lives. They believed they mattered, that their lives mattered. We, on the other hand, knew that we only mattered to each other, that as far as everyone else in the world is concerned, we were irrelevant, nuisances that could easily be gotten rid of without too great a sense of loss. Everyone who had ever loved us had died, everyone we mattered to had been sent to the gas chambers. All we had left were our lives and they were cheap. Death is no mystery; death means an end to starvation, an end to beatings, an end to the daily grind at the workshop. We knew we were going to die, we just wanted to delay it for as long as possible.

So we kept on working and every day was death. The airmen told us what to do and we did it. We were always afraid, always afraid of being beaten, of what the SS guards would do to us but we knew we had to just keep on working. It was hard for us to be children and to work the way we did with nothing to eat and not enough sleep. The British airmen were kind though, even occasionally sharing some meagre bits of food with us, and it made a difference.

We all worked in a large long room with a lot of other people, many of whom were children.   In some areas they were making clothes, and in others, boots. We would stack the metal plates and put them on the wooden shelves that line the walls.

Day in and day out, the monotony of the job was more demoralizing that the cold and the lack of food. There were no breaks, just continual work back and forth, and walking around constantly were the SS guards with their batons at the ready.

However, we still had our occasional jobs cleaning the mess and helping in the kitchen which continued to provide us with some extra sustenance and kept our spirits up. And then there were the British airmen. One day Norman dropped a plate on the floor and as Erhardt bent to pick it up, he said very quickly: "We had a parcel yesterday and we have some food for you."

Immediately he stood up. Erhardt saw a small package under the table. Pretending to fumble for the plate he opened the package and found some bread and chocolate. He took a small amount and quickly put it in his mouth, taking care to keep the package hidden against the leg of the bench.

Erhardt got up slowly, holding the plate, and checked to see where the guards were. When he was sure no one was looking he said a quiet thank you to Norman and indicated the location of the food parcel to us. One by one we ducked down on the pretext of picking up fallen bits of metal and feasted on bread and chocolate while the airmen watched out for us.

Norman was clearly impressed with us and said something to the other airmen that we could not understand. They nodded.

"You are fighters. The members of the underground are watching you. They can use kids like you."

An underground, here in Auschwitz? A resistance to the might of the German army right here? It was unimaginable but thrilling. We had been very happy stealing for ourselves, and had developed cunning and strategies to prevent being caught by the SS. But we had never thought of including anyone else or indeed of joining up with any other group.

Erhardt was very distrustful. The airmen had been very nice in sharing food but he wasn't sure whether they could be trusted. He had evidently heard rumours of spies for the guards who pretended to be friendly only to get information. That night outside the latrines, he expressed his concern. Mikhail was adamant that they were being honest.

"I can feel it, Erhardt" he insisted. "We don't have to worry about them. You know I am right about people. I picked Bernard and you, didn't I?"

We had a lot to think about. If the underground movement existed, we wanted to be a part of it, after all, we had nothing to lose. We risked our lives every day in Auschwitz, we figured we might as well die doing something important or at least trying to. Mikhail and I were excited by the adventure of it all but perhaps Erhardt, being older, understood more than us what was at stake for he was quieter than usual, even ignoring Mikhail's games. That we had been noticed thrilled us but obviously worried him, for if the underground had noticed us, surely the SS guards would have noticed as well. It all came down to what the airmen had in mind and whether or not they could truly be trusted. It was a difficult judgement call for such a young boy.

A few days later we were put to the test. Norman turned to Erhardt and told him about a package under the bench. He asked him to go and hide it, but not to tell anyone, including them. They didn't want to know any more about it.

The package was in an area not far from where the airmen were working. It consisted of two small tin boxes, each the size of a sardine can. Erhardt kept a lookout for the guards and at the safest moment signalled to us. I walked over to the spot, ostensibly to sweep the floor with a broom, but I hid the tins under the bristles. I swept the tins towards Mikhail. With Erhardt's body shielding us from the guards' vision, Mikhail and I picked up the tins and slipped them between some plates we were stacking. We carried the plates towards the shelves without breathing, expecting a guard to stop us at any minute. I can still feel that fear burning the back of my neck. Time had almost stopped. We placed the plates on the shelf, sliding the tins out and wedging them between the wall and the shelf. Then we walked back to the work area where we continued to stack plates for the rest of the day.

Those packages turned out to be small tins of explosives that had been made in the camp. Years later I was to read of the bravery of the women who worked in the ammunition plant who had managed to smuggle small amounts of gunpowder into the camp; of the prisoner who managed to create the explosives; of the loyalty and bravery of all those who resisted losing hope and fought back, even at the cost of their own lives. The sheer courage of these men and women has humbled me and made me so proud of our small contribution.

We hid the tins around the factory because we could not hide them in our clothing sufficiently to escape detection in the event of a search. We never discussed what had occurred, not once, not even in our bunk that night or on any other nights. You never knew who might be listening in Auschwitz.

TEN

WINTER BROUGHT WITH IT FREEZING NIGHTS, bitter mornings and shortened workdays. It also brought the doctors. One day a small dark man wandered in to the workshop, spoke rapidly to the SS guard and walked towards us with the eyes of the guard fixed firmly upon his back. We had seen him around the workshops before and he had always taken a few boys with him. They never spoke of what they had seen or where they had been. We would sometimes see him talking to Norman and the other airmen, but we were always out of earshot. This time, though, he looked straight at us, and then at Norman.

He shook his head sadly for we were a terrible sight: thin, dirty, and covered with sores and bruises, our teeth falling out and our gums bleeding.

He introduced himself as Dr Pasche. He said he had clearance from the guard to take us to do some work for him at Birkenau, carrying shoes and spectacles. We immediately looked to Norman for reassurance and when he gave us the very slightest nod of approval we relaxed a little.

"Dr Pasche tells us that we have to be back before 2pm. That means we will be out for most of the working day!" Mikhail was obviously pleased to have a break from the workshop and it took a sharp nudge from Erhardt to keep him quiet.

The doctor fell silent as we passed some guards who stopped him to examine the card he offered. "This card has been issued by Dr Mengele," he explained after they have moved on. "He is one of the chief doctors here. He is very ruthless. I work with him. I want to tell you some things about what goes on here. One day you boys might get out of here and I want you to remember what I have told you. I want you to tell the world what went on. This is why I work for the resistance movement and I want you three to do the same, so that this will never happen again, not to anyone.

On our journey to Birkenau he talked more openly.

"Listen carefully," he continues intently. "Auschwitz is, as you know, a work camp. Here they work you to death, and they feed you very little, as you well know. Birkenau, where we are heading now, is an extermination camp. You boys survived the selection on the ramp. That was the first selection. There will be others, but you will survive, I know it.

"I have a friend here, we both work with Dr Mengele; you will meet him soon. His name is Dr Nyiszli. Sometimes he will come for you like I have. He will tell you what is going on with the experiments and Dr Mengele. We want you boys to remember what we tell you. In return we will try and make sure that you get some extra food or clothing. It won't be much but it will be the best we can do."

We listened in silence as he talked. Occasionally guards or patrols stopped us but the magic card was shown and we were ushered on. For the first time we were hearing about what was really going on in Auschwitz. It was appalling, and we were terrified. It was like coming face to face with the *dybbyk*, a fictional monster, it was finding out that the nightmare you had had the night before was, in fact, real. We had heard whispers and rumours about Birkenau, we had seen the flames from the chimneys at night and the belching smoke during the day. Now we were going to confront it, the very thing that robbed us of our families, that disturbed our sleep, that made us obedient. We walked through rows and rows of identical buildings contained by the double electric fences that surrounded the whole area. We passed the entrance of the camp with the now infamous *Arbeit Macht Frei* arched ironically overhead.

"You probably don't remember much about your arrival," resumed Dr Pasche. But he was wrong. I remembered everything and the memory was painful. I saw Mikhail and Erhardt also flinch in memory of their arrival. However none of us said anything, we just let Dr Pasche continue.

"The group that was sent left was marched off five abreast flanked by SS soldiers and their dogs. They had no idea where they were being taken. They thought they were being taken to the baths, so they didn't even mind undressing. Their clothes were hung up and their shoes tied together. Then they were killed by gas and put into the ovens. I will tell you more in time. When there are a lot of bodies and the crematoria cannot cope, the pyres are used. "

He stopped talking as we approached a big white farm-style house surrounded by a large well-maintained courtyard. It looked just like any old country house backed by forest.

"Stay close to me," warns Dr Pasche. "If you don't you will find yourselves going through there and never coming back. That is where they go, thinking they are going to the baths. "

That warning did the trick and any thoughts we had of wandering off were instantly banished. The fear in Dr Pasche is palpable.

"There is a pile of clothes, glasses and shoes there. That's all that is left of the last group of people who did not make the first selection. I want you to pick them up and take them to the courtyard over there. That's the crematoria yard; the *sonderkommondos* there will take the stuff from you. See that man there, in the striped camp uniform?"

We saw a small dark man sorting through some shoes. We nodded.

"He is a Greek Jew and has been here for a very long time. He is one of the few prisoners allowed into the house here. He is a friend of mine."

Erhardt sensed our fear and I wondered if his thoughts matched mine. My parents would have left their shoes in a pile just like this. I shuddered visibly, so blinded by that thought that I was unable to see the opportunity.

He seemed to regret his impatience immediately and continued with more gentleness: "It is starting to get cold and we don't have shoes. Mikhail, don't you remember how cold it was last winter? Everyone got even more sick than usual. We are going to get out of this place and we need to take care of ourselves until we do."

I felt ashamed. Erhardt was right; we needed to see this as an opportunity. Mikhail still look scared and worried and to tell the truth, I too was frightened but I didn't want to risk Erhardt's scorn again. Instead I concentrated on the possibility of sneaking my feet unnoticed into a pair of shoes and keeping an eye on the armed guards sitting around the yards. They seemed to be relaxed but I felt as though they were watching our every move.

"This stuff gets sorted and taken to the *Kanada*," Dr Pasche informed us. "The *Kanada* are those huge storage buildings towards the back of the parade ground. They house all the stuff taken from the inmates of the camps and I think that it is sold all over Germany. Certainly all the officers take clothes and things for their wives and children. Have you come across our Beautiful Angel yet?"

We looked blankly at him for a moment and then Erhardt said ruefully, "Oh I know who you mean! Irma Griese. Don't you remember, Bernard, she is the one who did the last selection, the very smart one with the whip and the rope?"

"The bitch?" I ask.

"Why 'the bitch'?" asks Dr Pasche with a small smile.

"Well, she came onto the parade ground one day after roll call with a long rope. Two officers held the rope and all the boys who went under the rope were put onto the back of a truck and never returned. We know selections happen a lot here, so that wasn't so bad, but this woman decided to comfort the boys who were all crying and carrying on and she told them not to worry because they were going to soon be with baby Jesus!"

"We are Jewish, baby Jesus is not going to be of any comfort to us!" sneered Mikhail. "So we call her The Bitch. We hate her."

Dr Pasche worked in silence for a while. Then he said: "Were those the boys that called out their names as they were being driven off?"

"Yeah," answered Erhadt gravely. "It was weird. They called out their names; they had not forgotten who they were. Sometimes we see the most amazing things in this place."

"I heard about them. They were very brave, very dignified. So that was one of **her** selections. Well, where do you think she gets all her lovely outfits? She has the pick of Europe's most fashionable design houses right here!" There is no joy in Dr Pasche's laughter.

"What happened to all the people who wore these clothes?" I asked Dr Pasche.

"They were brought into this courtyard, and told to undress. Men, women and children. Then they were ushered out through this corridor in the house and into the thicket of trees behind. At the end of that you can see two huge pyres. They are massive holes in the ground, 100-150 yards long, 9 yards wide and 3 yards deep. The fire within burns very hot and very strong. Today, the people were mainly Jewish. They were upset and screaming and crying. The SS soldiers were bashing and cursing them. They were taken to the edge of the pyre and then shot so that they just fell into the fire. It didn't matter whether they were alive or not.

"Dr Mengele was here today. Don't worry, he is no longer here! But even he was horrified by what he saw. It's strange, but here is a man who can commit the most horrific human experiments being moved by the suffering of those people. Not that he did anything to stop it, though. Miklos, that's Dr Nyiszli, is convinced that Mengele has a heart. Perhaps he believes in his warped way, that his experiments will be worth something to someone one day."

He looked at us and saw that we were no longer following his train of thought. He smiled. "Don't worry, there is time for you boys to learn and understand everything. This is indeed a world gone mad."

We worked hard and Dr Pasche managed to help us procure a pair of shoes each. He warned us to take good care of them, as he knew how precious they were and that someone was bound to try and steal them. During the course of the morning we were joined by Dr Nyiszli, the one that Dr Pasche had spoken about. We could tell immediately from his accent that he, too, was not German.

"So, Andre," he says, "These are the boys I have heard about." Dr Pasche introduced us solemnly. "They are good boys – very brave and very smart. They will really be an asset."

"Good," says Nyiszli. "Now it is time for you boys to get back to the *Buna*. It is quite a walk and you have to be there before 2pm to make your afternoon roll call. Hopefully you will also get something to eat!" He laughed at his own joke.

As we walked back, the doctors talked and pointed out various buildings, telling us about experiments and autopsies, about how some people were taken into the hospital and never seen again, about bodies and body parts being shipped to medical institutions for further study. They also told us about Mengele and how, although they work closely with him, they cannot prevent anything from happening. They told us more about the resistance within the camp and how it works.

By the time we got back to our barracks I knew I had already forgotten more than half of what they had said. I was confused, incredulous and more frightened than ever before. It is one thing to face death, but to face painful experiments is something different. I had experienced the pain of constant beatings, but this sounded like more than I could bear and I said as much to Erhardt and Mikhail.

Mikhail's blue eyes were bright with reflected fear, and he was anxiously and nervously picking at a sore on his arm. Erhardt looked as resolute as ever. "We will get through whatever they choose to do to us and we will get through it together, so don't worry. We have people we can trust and they will help us. Look at the airmen and now the doctors. We will be okay. But let's not talk about this in front of anyone else."

The other residents of the barracks were returning from their day's work at the workshops around the *Buna* – the chemical workshops, the synthetic rubber plant, and the metal shop where we work making plates and reinforcements for the army. All in all, the German and Polish industrialists had a huge force of labour and expertise to draw upon. The strangest thing was that some of the most qualified people who had spent their lives in industry were doing the most menial jobs while others with little or no education and experience were given positions of great importance and responsibility. Such was the upside-down world of Auschwitz.

ELEVEN

OUR FEARS ABOUT BEING USED for experimental purposes were not unfounded given our status and the nature of our environment. We had heard on the Auschwitz grapevine that horrific things were being done to children, especially to twins. But until Dr Pasche had confirmed it they had really been only vague whispers and, being so caught up in ourselves until now, we had paid very little attention to the rumours. The three of us had existed in a cocoon, nourishing each other, giving strength and consolation when needed. We had built walls around us, walls to protect, both to keep ourselves in as well as others out. We had let in the British airmen because they were useful, giving us food and information. Now, the two doctors had penetrated our defences and it seemed that there was an entire network of people around who were doing what we were doing and more.

Erhardt was adamant however that we were not to trust too much or rely too much on anyone else. His reasoning was sound. They could die very suddenly and if we were too dependent upon them, we would die shortly after. We had already lost our families, he explained, we were not to make ourselves vulnerable to any other losses. But it was hard. Mikhail and I, less suspicious and that much younger than Erhardt, warmed under the interest of the doctors and the airmen. We admired their bravery and courage, we were impressed with their apparent power, with the ability of the doctors to move freely around the camp, or so it appeared, with the respect the SS guards showed towards the airmen, knowing they were under the eye of the International Red Cross. Our obvious admiration of them annoyed Erhardt who, with the cynicism of the disillusioned, reminded us that they were as vulnerable to the whim of the SS, to hunger, death and disease as any one of us.

One morning all the young boys were singled out after roll call and told they were volunteering for a special mission. This was devastating news as one of the advantages of the kind of work we were doing was that the workshop, although vast, was warmer than most, the heat being generated by the machines and the wasted bodies that operated them. All during the summer, if Mikhail and I had complained about the stifling heat and stuffiness, Erhardt used to say just think how warm this place will be in winter. And now it was nearly winter and we were being sent elsewhere.

"What are they going to do with us?" asked Mikhail in dismay.

"I don't know," replied Erhardt, "just stick close together and say nothing."

We were lined up in rows of three so we did get to stay together. On either side of the long column marched SS guards with two at the back and two at the front. They marched us out of the camp past the looming double fence upon which earlier I had seen a man hurl himself in desperation before being set upon by the ubiquitous ever-eager dogs.

There was no chance to talk, as conversation of any kind was strictly forbidden and punishable by immediate beatings. The tension in the air was palpable. We had all seen groups of inmates being taken out into the forests and not return. We had sometimes heard shots. We knew that in Auschwitz there were many ways for a Jew to die.

We walked for about one or two miles east of the camp in total silence. The morning was clear but cold. The extreme humidity of the summer had given way to a damp coldness that seeped under your skin, got into your bones and made itself known in the form of a constant ache. The forest air was cruel in all its pre-winter sweetness. It insulted our senses and mocked our foul-smelling lice-ridden bodies.

Eventually we came within sight of a large barn. At least we are going indoors, I thought. It also meant that we were not going to be shot. We were marched inside. The barn was cavernous and cold. We were all ordered to strip and then sorted into groups. We stood there shivering with cold and fear.

"I'm so cold!" I said when the guards were not looking.

"Me, too! What are they going to do to us?" asked Mikhail timorously.

We waited in silence for the guard to look away.

"I have no idea" replied Erhardt finally, "but these are some of the doctors from the camp."

"Shh!" I warned.

"Listen to that screaming from the others. I'm frightened. I don't want them to hurt me!"

"Just be brave, Mikhail. Remember don't show them any

weakness because if you do **you** will be selected for the ovens next time.

"Both of you, bite on your lower lip if they hurt you, or clench your fists, anything, just don't show them you're scared or in pain."

The guards barked out their orders and we complied.

A group of boys at various stages of adolescence, stripped of all but their dignity, shivering in the cold. Unable to meet each other's eyes, our fear as naked as our bodies, trying desperately to be brave. Some were crying silently, others murmuring prayers and songs of comfort from another life.

"You, come here!"

We were summoned by one of the guards and ushered towards a table where the doctors were waiting with an array of sharp instruments neatly laid out on a table in front of them. The instruments shone in the soft morning light that came in from a high-up window. Silver shards bounced off the tables onto the bleak walls, knifing through the gloom. The air was electrified by the palpable terror of the boys. One of the doctors checked our numbers against his notes. Erhardt was first. We watched alarmed as he examined Erhardt's penis and testes. Erhardt stared intently at the window close to the ceiling. He did not move or blink or flinch, it was almost as though he was no longer there. He was no longer occupying his body but travelling through that window and into the forest, deep into the green, dark forest through time and space.

The doctor made some notes and moved onto the next boy while another doctor stood in front of Erhardt. Obscured from my vision by the first doctor, I only saw the flinch as his body stiffened. The doctors moved down the line of boys and I began to feel the panic choking me. NO! I wanted to scream, this cannot be happening, why are they doing this! But there was no way to escape. Guards were all around us, they had guns and batons. I had seen what happened to boys who did not co-operate, we all had. None of us was prepared to risk a bullet to the back of the head, after all there were many of us, plenty to spare. I kept still, I could hear Erhardt's voice in my head repeating over and over: "Don't do anything to draw attention to yourself, don't resist, just go along with whatever they do."

It wasn't easy. Every instinct told me to run and hide, but I knew I couldn't, there was nowhere to go, I had to obey, and I had to submit. I was ashamed, we all were. We felt dirty, defiled in some way. I wondered what I had done wrong.

The doctor did not look at me; I was invisible, incidental. He lifted my penis, prodded my testes, made some notes. It was as though I was not there at all. I remembered how Erhardt had made himself disappear by focusing on the window and I tried to do the same. In my mind I was climbing out of that window and standing on the roof of the barn. The forest lay before me, a sea of swaying green, deep, dark and safe. I buried my self in the shadows of the trees until a sharp pain took my breath away and made me cry out involuntarily in pain and shock.

"Shut up, swine!" yelled a guard materialising behind me. The doctor glanced up at the guard. "Hold him still!" he barked, "Make sure he does not move."

The guard held me in a vice; one great arm around my chest while another guard came up and held my legs apart. The doctor completed the injection of fluid into my scrotum. The noise in the barn was deafening, the screams echoed from all around. I felt myself sinking into a black hole of pain; I couldn't breathe. My chest felt as though it was going to burst. As the pain began to subside I realised that the guard had put his hand over my mouth to muffle my screams. The noise had come from me.

I knew I was shaking, in shock and in fear. My legs felt weak, I was worried that I wouldn't be able to stand. Another doctor approached me.

"Do you have any night-time emissions?" he asked brusquely.

"What?"

The blow from the guard was hard and swift. "Answer the question!"

"I, I....er....."

What did they want from me? What emissions? I was afraid to answer and afraid not to. My scrotum was throbbing and it felt as though my testes where about to burst. My body was burning in confusion, anger and pain. I had to give an answer.

"No!" I managed to blurt out praying it was the right one.

"If you do, I want to know about it next time we see you." The doctor moved on to the boy who was standing ashen faced next to me.

The guard motioned me to the clothing pile. "They are done with you," he said. "Get dressed and join the others in the ranks."

Erhardt was standing there, already dressed and very pale. "Are you okay?" he asked. I looked away. Slowly I gathered my clothes and pulled them on. I had no words.

"Bernard, look at me!"

I shook my head, burning with shame and pain, and kept

my gaze firmly on the ground.

"Bernard...." He watched as the guard made his way towards us.

"Hurry up, you Jewish pigs. It's time to go back. Now!"

"Get into line, quickly! Move, move, move!"

I was grateful for the distraction of the guard, for not having to meet Erhardt's eyes. I lined up quickly and fixed my eyes firmly upon the ground. Mikhail tried to squeeze my hand, I pulled away quickly.

Whips, batons and boots, the tools of the guards' trade in Auschwitz, ensured that we were suitably lined up in our ranks. Some of the boys had died during the various procedures. Some were covered in blood. Some were to stay in the infirmary for a while. We were greatly diminished in number and very subdued on the walk back to the barracks. Bandy-legged, every step agony, every step a reminder of that humiliating and painful experience, we walked towards the little solace offered by a draughty barrack, a dirty straw mattress and a rag of a blanket. Not even the oblivion of sleep would provide an escape for us tonight.

I did not lift my eyes from the ground. I could not look at either Mikhail or Erhardt. I was broken inside, I felt dislocated, no longer intact. A shift had occurred, I too had been irrevocably altered.   I was ashamed, ashamed at what they had done, ashamed at how I had reacted, ashamed at how I was feeling now. I was nothing, I was dirty, I was an animal, what did I expect?

When we finally got back to the barracks, I crawled onto my bunk, forsaking even the limited freedom of the latrines for the oblivion of sleep. But even that was denied for the pain increased rather than decreased during the night. Even Mikhail was silent that night, interested in neither the rats nor tormenting the other inmates with talk of food and water.

"Bernard, listen to me," said Erhardt quietly late into the night, "it doesn't hurt any less but it does get easier. I don't know what they hope to find out with these experiments but don't let them break you. We are going to get out of this place, remember. We are going to go to America and become engineers, right? Just don't give up. Don't give up, ever."

Under the chilling onslaught of the northern winds, the rapidly dropping temperatures were providing challenges of another sort for the great German army, particularly the navy. It had come to the attention of the medical establishment at Auschwitz that the sailors would have a better chance of survival if more were known about the nature of hypothermia. To that end a new dimension of cruelty was added to our ever increasing humiliating experiences.

This time when we were taken out of the gates we were herded northwards for about eight kilometres. Once again the escort prevented any kind of escape: guards in the front, at the back and on the sides accompanied by vicious dogs trained to attack inmates on command. The road was rough and narrow. At one point the trees formed a canopy across the road.

"Where are we going now?" asked Mikhail. "Are we going for more injections?"

"I don't think so, this is a different direction," answered Erhardt, "Don't worry, it can't be any worse that what we have already been through!"

"Will it hurt?"

"Everything in Auschwitz hurts," he answered.

"I wish we still had our shoes. My feet are really hurting." I said softly as I gingerly placed my swollen feet on to the stony ground.

"Have you forgotten how badly the shoes hurt?" asked Erhardt irritably. "It's just as bad to wear them as it is to go barefoot."

"At least we got some extra rations for them," said Mikhail characteristically finding a positive aspect in everything.

"I don't think the sores on my feet will ever heal, though," he continued ruefully. "They are oozing puss. It's really disgusting."

"I am so cold," I complained, "I just hope that Norman will have some chocolate for us again when we return to the workshop. No matter what they do, I will just dream about chocolate!"

The airmen had been sympathetic when we told them about the barn and the next day had managed to smuggle us some chocolate in an effort to cheer us up. "Don't let them get you down," Norman had said when the guard was not in earshot, "there is a lot worse going on here."

I couldn't in my wildest dreams imagine anything worse than those injections, but his words returned to me on that walk towards the lakes. Could this be worse than what we had already been through?

We had been taken back to the barn numerous times, each time following the same procedure and each time they asked the same stupid questions. It did not get any less painful, but Erhardt was right, it did get easier. Eventually, Mikhail and I were able to leave our bodies in the same way that Erhardt did. So many boys died there, I think he saved our lives. I often wondered how he knew that trick but did not dare to ask. I could never speak to him of those experiments, the prodding and the poking, the humiliation. As horrific as they were, they seemed trivial next to what was being done to some of the other boys. We heard later from Dr Nyiszli of hormone injections, castrations, and burnings with X-rays. In comparison, we were lucky. I kept praying that our luck would hold out.

We walked quietly, acquiescing to the right of the Nazi doctors to use us as they saw fit. In spite of everything, I still felt proudly German. I still believed that whatever was being done was really being done for the good of the Fatherland. I mentioned this once to Erhardt after a particularly painful session in the barn. He looked at me strangely.

"Do you really believe that the experiments they are doing have some value?"

"But...why would they be doing them otherwise?"

"Because they can."

I couldn't accept that and began to argue.

"If anything," he replied, "They are trying to to prove the inferiority of the Jewish people."

"To prove that to whom?" I said not understanding.

He shrugged and said, "Don't worry about it, it is useless, get some sleep."

I recalled that conversation later in the day when we were walking back to the camp. It **had** all seemed so pointless, so useless.

The guards had marched us to a small water hole and circled it. They ordered us into the water, clothes and all.

"I can't believe this," muttered Erhardt, "What do they want from us now?"

The melting snow off the nearby mountains fed the underground rivers, which appeared every now and again as small lakes on the surface. The water temperature was constantly just above freezing, even in summer. Every fibre of our beings resisted immersion.

"It's one way to get clean," joked Mikhail screwing up his face as he apprehensively eased himself into the water.

I felt the prod of a baton in my back, lost my footing and slid into that icy depth. I yelled out in surprise before the shock of the cold took my breath away. All around me boys were screaming and jumping up and down with cold.

"Look at my hands," yelled Mikhail over the mayhem, "They are blue with cold!"

"Your lips are blue, too!" I yelled back through chattering teeth.

"So are yours!" laughed Mikhail. "I am so cold."

A large car pulled up with some of the medical staff. I watched as they conversed with the guards and then they began to call out our numbers. I listened carefully for mine. It was easy to miss your number being called with all that noise and mayhem, however to do so meant a certain beating. It just wasn't worth it.

Finally I heard my number.

"111404!"

I scrambled out of the water, evidently not fast enough for I caught a blow from a baton on the side of my head. Shivering and more than a little dazed, I stood as still as I could while my body temperature was taken and my heartbeat monitored. Standing in the sunshine was sheer heaven until I was ordered back into the water. A well-aimed and very well-timed kick from one of the guards ensured no possible chance of argument. I heard their laughter as the icy water reclaimed me. This procedure was repeated every 10 minutes or so until the medical personnel returned to their car and drove off.

And then it was over. We stood, shivering and miserable in our ranks, ready for the long walk back to the camp.
"There are bodies in the water!" yelled one of the guards. "You boys go back and get them out. You will need two boys for every body so that you can drag them back to the camp."

Mikhail and I were ordered back into the freezing water. We reached in and grabbed a young boy by the arms. He was no more than ten years old and as light as a feather. His lips were blue. He had probably died from the cold. There was no flesh on his body, just loose skin and bone, so he did not have even the remotest chance of maintaining any body-heat whatsoever. We dragged him out slowly, feeling the resistance from his waterlogged clothing. We were weak ourselves, but the energy expended helped to warm us up. We hitched our arms under his shoulders and allowed his body to drag all the way back to camp.

Throughout the experiment, no one bothered to explain what the purpose was, no one thought to ask if we minded doing it, no one showed any remorse over the poor boys who froze to death or drowned in the process. And yet I needed to know that we were suffering for a higher purpose. My father had told me we were going to help the fatherland, he had never lied to me before. I still needed to believe that we were helping somehow. That this was not just a colossal waste of life and time.

Cold, shivering and carrying the body of a drowned boy between us, we made our way slowly and painfully back to the barracks to be rewarded with a bowl of watery soup and some stale black bread. I kept remembering the taste of chocolate.

TWELVE

I ONCE HEARD OF AN OLD CHINESE CURSE that wishes you to live in interesting times. Perhaps if I had been able to explore my Jewish heritage I would find the equivalent sentiment expressed in either Yiddish or Hebrew for it is a saying borne of great suffering, something that we Jews are very familiar with. During that first winter of 1944, life in Auschwitz became very interesting and not in a very good way.

The fear of being killed in the forest by a shooting party had now changed to the fear of dying from a botched castration or hypothermia. If death scared us, so did living for we were now always cold, hungry, thirsty and in pain. At least that was nothing new. The morning after the day at the lakes we had to drag out the bodies of the boys who had died either at the lake or during the night onto the parade ground for roll call. We were keenly aware that it could just as easily have been one of us. As we stood on that icy ground shivering in the bitter predawn air, the bright camp lights flooding down on our misery, Erhardt said ruefully, "At least our day had some variety!"

Mikhail laughed and then choked. He had developed a cough that was worrying all of us, not in the least because he was coughing at night and waking us up. "Perhaps the doctors can get us out of these experiments?" he asked hopefully.

"I don't think anyone can get us out of this," said Erhardt, "We just have to make it as best we can. The important thing is to stick together and support one another."

"Shh, here's the guard."

We stood still and quiet, our eyes fixed on our feet. Erhardt helped to hold up the lifeless body of a young boy. It meant nothing to us that this boy had once breathed and laughed and been loved. He was now an inconvenience, his death a punishment we had to endure. If the death cart did not come by this morning his body would become stiff and start to smell. Maggots and rats would feed off it and even if that alone would not be enough to let him be we would still have to drag him out every morning and somehow hold him up. Sometimes it would be days before the cart came. Of course it was a lot worse in summer, but there seemed to be so many more bodies in winter.

We were becoming inured to death and yet our own deaths seemed inconceivable. How, faced with that wall everyday, did we manage to not see it? Erhardt said the angels were looking out for us, and Mikhail and I believed him. Our angels were certainly working overtime. That and the fact that the doctors kept telling us that kids as skilled as we are would definitely not be beaten by Auschwitz. And we believed them, why wouldn't we? We had each other, and we had the three airmen, the two doctors and now the resistance all looking out for us. And all around us, the Nazi war machine carried on their business as usual: the armaments that were made being shipped out, and the trains arriving daily, more and more trains, laden with their human cargo, shipped into Auschwitz, taken straight to Birkenau, to the gas chambers and the ovens. And we would be there to pick up piles of spectacles, glasses, shoes and clothing and hand them over to the *kommondos* in charge who would take them to the *Kanada* for storage. And the doctors would tell us their tales of mass executions, experiments, hangings, and torture all the while saying: "Pay attention, you must remember for you will survive to tell the world. This must not be forgotten."

The seasons began to change once again and we noticed that the days were becoming longer. This meant that our workday was becoming longer too because we worked from sunrise to sunset. It meant less free time; it meant the return of the stifling humid air that provided such a good breeding ground for the many bacteria and viruses that cursed the camp. Above all it meant rot and decay. Life in Auschwitz going on pretty much as it always had. We knew we would have to battle against hunger, fear and thirst. We were taken into the forests, we worked in the workshop, we cleaned the mess and we peeled potatoes outside the kitchen.

Our time in the workshop with the airmen was becoming less frequent as the imaginations of Dr Mengele and his associates thought up more and more ways to utilise our young bodies for the betterment of the German people. They had stripped us of every dignity, even control over our own bodies.

And along we went without a fight, to the barn in the forest or to the lake, to the mess or the kitchen or the workshop. It was our life, our camp routine; we learnt to deal with pain and humiliation, with beatings, hunger, thirst and fear. We watched impassively as the adults around us fought with themselves and others, trying to remember what it was like to be important, to matter, trying to regain their self-esteem and confidence, trying to survive. We didn't bother, we were happy being nothing, unnoticed. Who cared if we were filthy and dressed in rags? Who cared if no one knew our names? Our mothers weren't around to take much notice. There was a certain amount of freedom in the lack of adult supervision. We avoided the guards. If we didn't draw attention to ourselves, they would leave us alone. We didn't hate them, they were just there, placing restrictions upon us that we learnt to circumvent, imposing rules that made no sense but we had easily accepted the lack of sense in Auschwitz. In fact we were all too young to have figured out the adult world anyway, even in peace, so we created meaning ourselves, our own understanding of hell. To steal, lie and cheat better than anyone else meant we would survive another day, and we prided ourselves on being the best thieves and liars that Auschwitz could spawn. The cleverer we were, the better off we were and we took care only of ourselves. We were shown no compassion and in turn did not demonstrate any. Sometimes quite the contrary.

"Hey, Erhardt!" Mikhail shouted one night when rations had been severely limited due to the Kapo spilling the soup. "Pass me the water."

"What water, do you have water?" echoed around the barracks. Water was such a precious resource and our primary battle was against the unbearable thirst that constantly plagued us.

"Shut up, Mikhail!" Erhardt replied angrily. "You know there is no water."

But it was too late; the other inmates would not believe him.

"You are lying, we know you have water," they cried.

"Share it with me, I won't tell a soul, I promise."

"Please, I am very ill, I need a drink."

"Please...."

"Look, I'm sorry," said Erhardt, glaring angrily at us for laughing, "We really don't have water. Mikhail is just being a fool."

Mikhail and I thought it very funny how easily the others could be duped. We had let slip once before that we had had an apple and the resulting chaos had kept us amused for days. We related the story with glee to Norman the following day while ostensibly picking up fallen plates and sweeping the floor. Norman shook his head sadly.

"What will become of you boys? What are you learning in this place?"

One morning in the workshop while things were carrying on as usual Norman dropped a plate on the floor, the signal that he wanted to talk. Erhardt bent down to pick it up.

Norman said quietly: "We are going to teach you boys to use the explosives."

Erhardt stood up quickly before he could attract the attention of the guards. He had a secretive look on his face and we could see he was bursting to tell us this latest news. When he saw that the guard had turned away he relayed the message with great excitement.

"Now this is what being part of a resistance means!" grinned Mikhail, "We get to blow things up!"

"Maybe we can blow up the barn where the doctors are?" I asked hopefully.

Norman overheard: "Ssh, you'll attract the attention of the guard, don't talk, just listen."

There was no safe place to discuss this latest development and we did not trust anyone anyway. Even the doctors were not to be trusted with this new information. Over the course of the next few weeks, whenever we could grab a few moments, Norman would explain the makings of an explosion. He would always end his instruction with the phrase: "Just remember: red to red, black to black." We slept at night with those words echoing in our brains like a mantra: Red to red, black to black.

In the workshop the next day Norman said to us: "What will you do?"

"What do you mean?"

"What do we have to do?"

"The wires, the wires!"

"Oh, that!"

"Red to red, black to black."

"Yes! Now, don't forget."

This went on for about four months and in that time we heard the exciting news that America had entered the war against Germany. The great America! Surely this meant the end to our pain and suffering. Throughout summer the German Army had seemed invincible, conquering more and more countries, moving closer and closer to world domination. The Jewish people, scattered all over Europe, were being herded into camps in Poland and Germany without causing too much of an outcry anywhere in the world.

We had survived winter under the most atrocious conditions had been subjected to the most awful degradations, been worked and starved half to death, but we had survived. And unseen to the world, the Nazi war against the Jews, Gypsies, homosexuals, and other 'undesirables' continued unabated.

Roll call, always a prime time for selections, became more treacherous than ever as more and more trains arrived with human fodder. The slightest infraction meant instant death; the ovens were working at full capacity, night and day.

In the barracks from our bunk at night we could see the fires from the chimneys burning. From my first lonely night in the camp the flames had mesmerised me. I would stare out at those flickering lights, remembering a burning stove in a very different kind of kitchen in a very different time. As the weeks turned into months and those into years, the faces in that kitchen began to blur but the sense of the fire remained the flames of that memory fanned by the flames from the Birkenau chimneys. And so I stared, night after night, until my eyes could no longer focus and the flames and the night sky, starless against the bright lights of the camp, blurred into one, and I, unable to resist any longer, would fall into a deep and troubled sleep.

One night as I was staring as usual at the flames I saw something I had never seen before. I called to Erhardt and Mikhail who were lying on the other side of the bunk.

"Come here and take a look," I said. "Tell me what you see."

"Take a look at what?" asked Erhardt impatiently because he was tired and wanted to sleep.

"The flames, there is something strange there."

"You are always staring at those flames, Bernard," said Mikhail. "That's what's strange. Don't you find it creepy? All those bodies burning."

"There is something different tonight, come and see."

The two of them scrambled over, and stared out the window towards Birkenau and the chimneys.

"Can you see it?" I asked impatiently

There was silence for a while, then Mikhail replied slowly: "You mean that strange glow around the flames?"

"Yeah."

"Couldn't that just be the reaction of the heat and the cold? Like steam or smoke or something like that?" asked Erhardt, forever the pragmatist.

We were watching white shapes like giant moths swirling around the flames. Attracted to and then repelled by heat, these shapes shimmied and danced, silhouetted against the empty sky.

"Let's ask someone else," I offered

We called over one of the other inmates to have a look.

"Do you see them?" we asked.

"I see the flames," was the reply.

"Do you see any white shapes?"

"What? Of course not! Is this one of your stupid tricks?"

We asked everyone on that night and on the other nights when we sat fascinated by the dance of the white beings and every time we asked we got the same response. No one seemed to see what we saw. No one else seemed aware of the ephemeral dancers surrounding the flames. We were in awe of the vision.

Perhaps we saw them because we were children, still willing to believe in salvation, in magic, in fairies and fables. Perhaps we saw what we wanted to see. Perhaps Erhardt was right, what we saw was merely the heat of the flames reacting with the cold of the night air, pushing out ashes into the steam.

It was many years later that I read of another account of this phenomenon.* The writer thought that what he was seeing was a heavenly apparition. He was a deeply religious man who described this vision as the angels of God guiding the souls of the Jewish people back to the Lord. Today, as a deeply religious man myself, well versed in the bible, I take comfort in that thought:

The purified souls of the children of Israel, sacrificed in the fires of Leviticus, being welcomed into the kingdom of God by His angels, while He prepares the land for his people. This thought has sustained me, has given my experience meaning. The Lord was preparing the land of Israel for His people and soon the survivors were going to return home.

---

* Stringer, Col *800 Horsemen* Col Stringer Ministries, Inc. 1998, Queensland

THIRTEEN

BEFORE WE COULD RETURN HOME there was a challenge the world had to face. There was the small matter of defeating Hitler and his Nazi army. With the help of the Americans and the Russians the great German war machine was having a spot of bother, at least that was what Norman relayed to us.

Dr Pasche came to pick us up as regularly as he could, passing on messages to Norman and filling us in on the details of the Auschwitz death camp.

"The crematoria I am talking to you about today are Crematoria 3 and 4."

He would begin and we would know that it was time for the lesson and we were expected to pay attention.

"They were built after the 'Final Solution' was put in place, which was May 1941. About 360 bodies are cremated every half-hour so between all the crematoria and the pyre about 24,000 bodies are being burnt. The *Sonderkommandos* of which I am a part, work 12 hour shifts. Big trucks like the 'Brown Toni', which you have seen collecting the bodies from the barracks, are lined up at the Crematoria gates to cart away the ashes which are used as fertiliser for the surrounding farms or dumped into the Vistula River.

"Do you boys remember some of the other things I have told you? Remember that when the Crematoria are overtaxed like now in the summer of '44, the white house and the pyre are used?

"You boys are very brave. There are other brave people here too. There were some Greek Jews who were ordered to kill a group of Hungarian Jews. They refused to kill other Jews and resisted with terrible courage. So the German officers killed them first and then killed the Hungarians as well. Four hundred brave men were killed, but not for nothing. They stood up to the Germans; they retained their humanity and their dignity. Although the Germans killed the Hungarians anyway, at least the Greek Jews died knowing that they had offered some form of resistance. Like them, you boys must never give up nor give in to hatred. One day you boys will get out of this place and when you do, tell the world these stories, tell the world about the courage and dignity of the people imprisoned here."

We would listen intently, absorbing all the details, confident in the knowledge that we would be released from this place and would fulfil our obligation to record what he had told us.

One day Dr Pasche arrived at the workshop with another doctor we had never seen before. She approached us with an assurance unusual in a prisoner, emanating a sense of power. Her height gave her an imposing air, the way she carried herself suggested someone not to be trifled with, but her most arresting feature was her dark eyes that bored right into your very soul.

"This is Doctor Mitrovna," said Pasche.

We had heard of her. She had often intervened on behalf of a prisoner. A talented and respected surgeon before the war, she was useful to Mengele because of her skills and had therefore managed to survive so far. We learnt that it had been she who was relaying the messages to the Resistance from the Allied forces by way of a radio hidden in the *Kanada* and with the help of a mysterious Czechoslovakian whom we never met.

The two of them spoke to Norman for a while and then she turned to us and said: "Hello my boys, or should I say Dr Pasche's boys! We are all from many countries, I am from Russia and you three are German, but we all want the same thing and that is freedom. You boys are doing a good job; just remember to be very careful."

She smiled and walked away leaving us with the impression of having made another good friend.

Norman turned to us and said, "Listen, according to Dr Mitrovna, sometime today you boys are meant to be going back to the lakes. You might have noticed that things are getting a bit slack around here. There are not quite so many guards as before. We think things are beginning to go badly for the German army and all the reserves are being called up to fight at the front. There are not going to be quite as many soldiers guarding you as in the past.

"Do you remember where you hid the first lot of explosives?"

We nodded.

"Good. We want you to take the two packs of explosives and hide them under your shirts. Tuck them in if you can so they don't show. This is very risky and if you get caught you will probably be tortured and then hanged so if you don't want to do this we understand.

"Now be very careful. They are not searching everyone because they don't suspect anything, but you never know. Hide the explosives well because we don't know exactly when you will be going.

"When you are called, you will be escorted with a lot fewer guards than before. Make sure you are in the middle of the rank, not at the beginning, or at the end. You will be walking in threes as usual so stick together. Apparently there is a bend in the road followed by an avenue of overhanging trees. When you get to that spot, just drop off carefully. You will be met in the forest."

We had been to the lakes about a dozen times so we knew exactly the spot to which he was referring.

"Just do what you're supposed to do. If you get back we will be sure to have some chocolate for you." Norman smiled but he looked worried.

"Please be careful, don't do anything to make them suspicious, just be normal."

Erhardt and I agreed to hide the explosives, believing that we would have a greater chance at success than Mikhail who always had difficulty hiding his emotions. The responsibility was enormous. If we were caught we knew we would be tortured until we had told the SS where the explosives had come from. Not only that, all the boys assembled for the lake would somehow be implicated and punished, regardless of their involvement. I wasn't sure whether I could withstand any form of torture. I desperately wanted to run away. Unfortunately, there was nowhere to run. I looked at Erhardt, he was calm. It was reassuring. I knew we had no choice, we had to try.

It wasn't long before the SS officers summoned us for a roll call. Nervously, I joined the assembled boys on the parade ground outside the workshop. I held my breath as the soldiers went through their usual procedure of abuse and counting. I waited until everyone was satisfied that the right number of boys had been assembled while the explosives seared my flesh generating a heat that I was sure would burn all those around me. I was certain that everyone could see my shaking hands, and that they all knew what I was carrying, could see the tiny package protruding out of the thin fabric of my shirt. I was convinced that I was being toyed with, played like a cat with a mouse, tantalised with hope, led into a false sense of security so that I would drop my guard.

Each time a soldier walked by, I anticipated a sudden movement, saw vividly before me the raised arm, felt the inevitable blow, and then watched helplessly as the tin of explosive rolled out into plain view of everyone. I felt the sweat prick the back of my shirt, bead on my forehead, and pour down my sides. I imagined the explosive as a great square box pressing outward against a shirt drenched in sweat. I imagined the guard roughly lifting my shirt to see the source of such a suspicious bulge. I felt the noose tightening around my neck as my legs kicked against the void.

We were counted and marched out of the camp.

"Mikhail, just don't muck up," warned Erhardt. "See those boys swinging on the gallows, if they catch us now, that's where we will be. Just for once, march properly!"

Mikhail grinned. Far from experiencing my paralysing fear,

Mikhail had pure excitement written boldly across his face: his cheeks were flushed and his eyes bright, luckily that could be explained away as a fever, a not so uncommon occurrence.

"Don't look so happy," I snarled sarcastically, angry at my own fear. "That really will attract attention."

Soon we were marching out of the camp and heading towards the forests. We had positioned ourselves in the middle of the file as instructed. There were guards in the front but none of the usual guards on the sides or amazingly enough at the back. We marvelled at the accuracy of the information received by the airmen.

It was very pleasant to be out of the camp with the light from the late summer sun dancing with the shadows cast by the softly swaying leaves. I sighed and imagined being able to walk freely along this path, stopping at will to pick a wildflower or crush a sweet smelling leaf in the palm of my hand. The soil was thick and rich and very marshy under our feet. Oozing with rotting leaves and decaying branches, the ground pulsated with life, while the ooze and decay of our bodies foretold only disease and death.

As soon as we came to the allocated spot, we discreetly dropped out of rank and melted into the shadows of the overhanging trees. We crouched down and slithered away watching the file close up neatly. Amazingly no one even looked our way or seemed to notice our sudden disappearance. The partisans had chosen the spot wisely: we simply vanished.

"Now what?" whispered Mikhail from under the cover of an overhanging bush.

"We wait," answered Erhardt softly and sure enough it

wasn't long before we heard a sound behind us and were being beckoned silently by three members of the Polish resistance, two men and a woman. We moved cautiously towards them, our hearts beating, the adrenaline coursing through our veins making us light headed and euphoric.

We moved off until we were some distance from the road.

"You got it?" hissed the woman. We nodded assuming it was the explosive they were after. I reached into my shirt to hand it over.

"No, no. Keep it," she said. "You have done good. Here."

From somewhere within her large coat she produced a small bundle.

"Eat, eat!" she said.

She carefully opened the bundle and offered its contents to us. Miraculously, inside were biscuits dusted with cinnamon and sugar. We stared in amazement, our eyes wide; unable to believe the treasure we were being offered.

"Eat, eat, you deserve it. You are brave boys."

We bit into the soft, crumbly surface very slowly, feeling it break up in our mouths into a thousand little taste sensations. Sweetness and spice exploded on our tongues. We had never tasted anything like this before. If this was the reward for smuggling explosives we were more than willing to risk torture and hanging every time! Then one of the others said something to her in what must have been Polish and she said: "Come, run, quick!"

We ran for a short distance and came to a river. Spanning the river was a railway bridge. "Here, give," the Polish woman commanded. We happily handed over the explosives and saw they had supplied the detonators. We saw the wires, red and black, and understood the teaching of the airmen.

"Red to red, black to black," murmured Erhardt.

"Ja, thanks," said one of the men with a smile as he connected the wires.

Under the supervision of the partisans, we placed those explosives carefully under the bridge. Being smaller than the adults we were able to squeeze into places they could never have reached enabling the bombs to be placed in the most effective positions.

Soon we heard the rumbling of a train coming from the opposite side of the bridge.

"Quick, back!" yelled the woman.

We ran for cover in the forest and crouched down under the bushes. The train appeared, moving inexorably slowly towards the bridge. Our timing had been perfect. The detonators were set, everything was ready.

As the train reached the bridge I watched as one of the partisans pushed the plunger. Instantly the bridge exploded before our eyes. Mikhail started jumping up and down screaming with excitement, "We did it, we did it!"

"Idiot!" yelled one of the men and pulled him down.

"Now, run!" they ordered.

We raced back to the road, laughing with excitement. "We did it, we did it!" shouted Mikhail over and over. "Did you see that bridge go up? Wasn't that fantastic?"

Crouching down in the bushes we had to wait a little while before the boys were due to return from the lakes. While we were crouching under the bushes, I turned to Erhardt. "The detonator went off too early," I said, "the train managed to brake."

One of the men overheard me. "At least we blew up the bridge," he reminded me. "That makes a difference. You boys did well."

"Shh, here they come," said the woman.

We lay very still until the rear of the column was hidden by the bend in the road and then the partisans gave us a push and we melted back into line, rejoining the shuffling boys, trying hard to stay in step. We wanted to run and jump and dance. We were saboteurs! We were resistance fighters!

We neared the entrance to the camp, standing there were two SS officers counting us all in. We walked past, eyes fixed firmly on the ground, trying to look just as cold and miserable as the other boys.

"I am so thirsty," said Mikhail suddenly as we broke rank near the barracks. He dropped onto his knees in front of a large puddle that the setting sun had turned into liquid gold. Suddenly Erhardt kicked him hard and sent him sprawling.

"Have you gone crazy! You can't drink that water! It is contaminated. If you drink it you will die. You are such an idiot sometimes!"

"Sorry," said Mikhail sheepishly. "I forgot. I am just so thirsty."

Erhardt stared at him impatiently and then, seeing his crestfallen face and the look of pain, said remorsefully, "We'll check the tin in the latrines to see if there is any water for you. You should know better than to drink the water from the ground. How on earth will you ever manage without me?"

I looked at Erhardt startled. He had never before spoken about us not being together. We were a unit; we would always be together. Suddenly I was very frightened.

"What do you mean, Erhardt?"

"Nothing. Let's go and check our water supply. Also I have some bread from this morning. We can share it, after all, we should celebrate!"

Fourteen

I HAD NEVER SEEN MIKHAIL AS HAPPY as he was that moment when the bridge exploded; hidden in the bushes, jumping up and down with excitement, face glowing, eyes gleaming, he was for a few seconds a child again. We felt so strong, so powerful, so important.

The next day we were sent back to the workshop and there waiting for us were the British airmen with the promised pieces of chocolate.

"Do you know the effect of what you did?" asked Norman.

"No," replied Erhardt.

"We just did what you told us to do," I said.

"Well," smiled Norman. "There were German soldiers on that train and they were coming here to kill us all and hide the evidence of what was going on here."

"Why?" asked Mikhail

"Because that way they could say that all the people just disappeared."

"But we only blew up the track," I said, "The train managed to brake."

"That's okay," replied Norman, "It still slowed things down. The Russians are getting closer and closer; you can hear their guns already. It is only a matter of time. You boys have done well."

Norman was right, every night now the camp air-raid sirens would be going off, as Russian bombs came terrifyingly close and according to Norman, the partisans were managing to smuggle a lot of supplies into the camp for the Resistance. Terrified that we were going to be hit by a Russian or American bomb, at first we huddled on our bunks, unable to run, unable to sleep. We tried to imagine what it would be like to die from a bomb blast, wondered whether we should try and get a bottom bunk, we exhausted every possible image and option until eventually, we grew numb to the idea and apathy settled upon us once more.

But during the day our lives carried on as usual. We couldn't and wouldn't talk to anyone about the bridge explosion for fear of getting our friends into trouble and seemingly within hours it was as though it never happened and we were back to the tedium of trying to forage for food, staying away from the guards, and generally getting through the day alive. We had long since stopped making plans beyond the end of the day. It required too much energy. The tedium of the camp was hard to bear after so much excitement. Even Mikhail's seemingly endless source of enthusiasm had begun to wane as we trampled back and forth between Auschwitz and the workshop in Monowitz. And all around us German efficiency saw to it that the camp operated pretty much the same way with early morning roll calls, random selections, and assigned work details punctuated by brutal beatings and bashings.

The heat and humidity of summer had given way to the freshness of autumn and I noticed the leaves were absorbing the colours of the sun, radiating umbers, and ochres, burnt oranges and siennas. And ahead of us, another winter, another battle for survival against the cold, the lack of food and the illness that ravaged the camp. But everyone knew things were changing, it was in the noise of the guns coming closer and closer, it was in the demeanour of our guards, it was in the eyes of the inmates. Something was shifting underfoot, we felt it, sensed it, saw it, but we weren't quite ready to believe it, not yet.

One night the camp sirens went off as usual but this time we could see that all the lights were on which meant it could not possibly be because of enemy bombs. The camp was lit up so brightly I imagined it could be seen for miles from the sky. We were confused and once more frightened. The lights usually came on if there had been a break out and they would stay on until the inmates had been found. Then we would all be summoned to watch the execution as a lesson to anyone who thought that they too would try to escape. We would watch as the escapees would either be shot or hanged. Sometimes the bodies would hang for days on the gallows as a warning to anyone else. Usually the reprisals echoed throughout the camp, anyone with any connection to the escapees, whether in the same barracks or part of the same workgroup was also punished. It was a very efficient system punishing the collective for the behaviour of the individual. You thought twice about doing something when so many others would suffer the consequences. It also made inmates very suspicious of each other, watching one another guardedly to make sure that everyone towed the line, no one was willing to suffer for anyone else's stupidity or misguided sense of bravery.

We were not summoned to the parade ground for roll call; the door to the barracks remained locked. Excitement inside the barracks ran high; everyone had an opinion on what had happened. There had been a breakout. Maybe the Russians had entered the camp? Was this it? Was this liberation? When the kapos and some particularly irritated guards finally summoned us, we were none the wiser. We were just counted as normal and sent off to our usual places of work.

Later that day, Dr Pasche came into the workshop and spoke very quickly to Norman. I stared at him. Dr Pasche, normally so precise and dapper, was dishevelled and agitated. He was talking excitedly and rapidly, his frustration over using another language evident in his rapid hand movements. His usual calmness had been shattered and we needed to know why. The number of guards watching us in the workshop had diminished and we found that lately, as long as we appeared busy, we did not attract the attentions of anyone. Also, the noise of the various presses was enough to keep our voices from being overheard so we had been able to talk more than before. As soon as Dr Pasche moved off, choosing some other boys to take with him this time, we gathered around Norman.

"What's going on?" asked Erhardt. "Dr Pasche seemed very strange."

"Dr Pasche and Dr Nyiszli were locked in the gas chamber last night with about 200 other inmates who work that detail. Did you hear the sirens wailing all last night?"

We nodded, it had been impossible not to.

"Well, according to Dr Pasche some explosives, guns and

gasoline were found."

"Where?" asked Erhardt, praying it wasn't in our workshop.

"Don't worry, it wasn't here," said Norman assuringly, "It was in another part of the camp. But they have been searching the whole camp. It also appears that the wires of the fence were cut. How they managed that is anyone's guess. Anyway, everyone was locked up all night while they searched the camp and interrogated inmates.

"The doctors thought they had been taken to the gas chambers to be killed. They were very frightened. They waited all night for the gas to start, but it never did. Some of the men went mad in there. Dr Pasche said it was really terrible."

"We are going to have to be even more careful in future," said Erhardt thoughtfully.

"Let's get back to work before the guard comes round," cautioned Norman.

A few nights later we were woken suddenly by being attacked with whips and batons. A large group of SS officers led by the head of our barracks erupted into our dreams screaming, "Search the place!" "Get the Pigs out onto the parade ground then search this place from top to bottom!"

Terrified and blurry eyed, we filed past the guards, a gauntlet of whips and batons. In the mad shuffle to regain some kind of order, I managed to manoeuvre myself next to Erhardt and saw Mikhail doing the same thing.

"What is going on?" I yelled above the screaming and chaos.

"I don't know!" yelled back Erhardt.

Soon all the moving and shouting died down to a quiet whimpering and then all went still. The minutes became hours, and still we stood, in the dark, cold air, mesmerised by the flames from the chimney. Cinders and ash were falling all around us and the air smelled strongly of burning flesh. The ovens and the gas chambers were working around the clock.

Then suddenly it was over, we were sent back to the barracks, given the usual breakfast and told to go to the workshop. A thick heavy pall of smoke hung in the clear morning air.

Things seemed to get back to normal very quickly. As always in the camp it was business as usual. No explanations, no reasons, no information.

"Did they wake you up in the middle of the night?" asked Norman with a strange look on his face.

"Yes. Do you know why?"

We were all extremely curious.

Norman looked around to check on the location of the guard.

"Apparently during the night, sometime around midnight, we think a group of Russian partisans were able to get into the area near Crematorium One. Unfortunately we think they mistook the SS mess and kitchen for the Crematorium building because they were blown up."

"Did they get away? Was anyone hurt?" asked Mikhail anxiously.

"No-one got caught and no-one was hurt," whispered Norman. "They were lucky, but the camp guards are really angry. The war is not going well; the German army is suffering some heavy defeats and has a lot of casualties. Watch out for the guards."

We could see the guard coming over so we busied ourselves packing plates while Norman joined George and Edgar in operating the pressing machine. The guard berated us for a while and then wandered off to give some other poor soul a hard time. And so it went on, business as usual. We would be used as human guinea pigs at the lake or in the barns, we would be sent to the kitchen to peel potatoes, to the mess to clean up after the officers.

"What are they going to do to us today?" Mikhail would ask and then we would groan, "Oh, no! Not that again!"

But we never gave in, not really; there was that one time just before liberation but other than that we were strong. We would see the boys they put on those masturbating machines just drop, just die, right there in front of us. The absolute cruelty was beyond our belief. That they could do these things to us, that human beings were doing it to other human beings...and we would hobble back to camp with painfully swollen scrotums whimpering: "Don't bump me! Please, just don't touch me!"

We would see the boys in the water suddenly stop moving, losing the battle to stay warm. We would watch as the pain and fear disappeared from their faces and we would know that they were dead. We envied them that peace, we were angry with them for leaving us, and so we carried them roughly back to camp taking out our fear and frustrations on the skeleton that was probably once a well fed, well loved little boy.

We continued to supplement our diet of camp soup, coffee and black bread with whatever food we could scavenge from the mess, the kitchen or the airmen. Occasionally we were caught, sometimes even beaten, but mostly we managed to get away with it.

One morning we were assembled on the parade ground for the usual interminable and senseless roll call when the medical team showed up once again. This was always trouble. Two kapos and some doctors wielding a trolley came towards us.

"This looks ominous," I said nervously.

"Will this hurt?" asked Mikhail.

"Yes!" replied Erhardt and myself in unison.

"Well, what will I do?"

Erhardt looked at him in exasperation: "Just bite your lip like you always do."

It was our turn. I felt my arm being pulled forward roughly by one of the kapos. Almost instantly a needle was inserted into my most prominent vein. I watched with a mixture of fascination and horror as my blood turned the tube a deep red. My head began to spin, I could no longer feel my feet. I seemed to be watching from a great distance as my blood pulsated away from my body. I watched in horror as some boys collapsed on the parade ground and were left to lie there. Then it was over and I could hear Erhardt talking.

"Bernard, are you okay?

Bernard, can you hear me?"

"I'm fine," I replied slowly, regaining my equilibrium. "How are you and Mikhail?"

"We're okay," said Mikhail, "What are they going to do with our blood, Erhardt?"

"I don't know."

"They hate us so much, what do they want our blood for?"

Wasn't that ironic: Hitler's Aryan race needing the blood of the Jewish vermin to keep alive? Not only did they have our blood on their hands; they now had it in their veins.

FIFTEEN

THE REVOLT CAME IN THE EARLY PART OF OCTOBER that year, not very long after we had blown up the bridge. We heard the explosions in the middle of the day followed by the wailing of the sirens and machine-gun fire. We happened to be in our barracks having returned for the afternoon roll call. The doors were quickly locked from the outside. We had no way of knowing what was going on.

"Perhaps the Russians have invaded the camp," suggested Mikhail.

"Or it could be the partisans again, or a bomb."

We all huddled around the lower bunks speculating as to what was going on. We could see smoke through the window but not much else.

"I think something has happened to the crematoria," commented Erhardt matter-of-factly.

Shouts of "What! Let me see, let me see!" came from all over the barracks as people clamoured to see for themselves.

In the excitement of the moment, the inmates forgot the most important survival lesson of Auschwitz and Mikhail, Erhardt and I capitalised on the confusion and excitement to add another jacket, a new cap, and some bread to our supplies.

Suddenly, the door to the barracks burst open and in marched a ferocious looking group of guards with equally ferocious looking dogs. Mattresses consisting of a few pieces of dirty straw were overturned, bunks were moved, inmates were searched, every nook and cranny was thoroughly sniffed and inspected and still we did not know what was going on. Orders were barked in rapid German that made it hard to understand, even for a native. Then as suddenly as they had arrived, the guards left, bolting the door behind them.

For us, the crematoria were symbols of the might of the Nazi army and if they could, in some way, be damaged, it demonstrated that the seemingly invincible Third Reich was not so invincible after all. Our elation did not last long. We knew of Dr Pasche's involvement with the underground but we had not known that he had been directly involved in the blowing up of the crematorium. We learnt from Dr Mitrovna a few days later that Dr Pasche had been taken into the forest and shot along with a group suspected of being conspirators. She seemed disheartened, we assumed she was sad about the death of Dr Pasche. She explained that the revolt had not gone according to plan and that the reprisals were going to be severe. She warned us to take care and that she would not be seeing us again. She said there were still people who were looking out for us and that we must not lose heart.

We felt that familiar sensation of abandonment - once more we were alone. We had put so much faith in Dr Pasche and the resistance; we thought he was beyond reach of the camp system. It seemed that everyone we depended upon was going to leave us.

Norman tried to cheer us up, but he was also devastated by the loss. We had lost our connection to the underground, or so we thought.

The balmy months of autumn were swept away by the icy winds of winter and soon we were too worried about keeping warm and staying alive to dwell on the demise of Dr Pasche and the lack of activity from the underground. Injured soldiers began to appear in the camp, and the gypsy area, which was quite near our barracks, was suddenly emptied. I had developed a fear of the gypsies over the years. They would tease and torment us as we walked by on our way to the workshop. Every now and again, one of them would start a fight with a Jew and beat him to death. The guards never stopped the fights but seemed to revel in the spectacle of it. Like the spectators of a cockfight, they would arrange bets on who would be victorious. I quickly learnt to avoid their barracks, sometimes going quite out of my way to do so.

Then we woke one morning to find the gypsy camp suddenly deserted, the occupants mysteriously vanishing overnight, men, women and children. As terrified of them as I was, it was strange to have this emptiness within the camp. They were bright, loud and colourful. They never did any work as such and seemed to be there to inflict more humiliation upon us, but their disappearance was ominous. It was as though the Nazis were slowly and methodically getting rid of all traces of prisoners in Auschwitz. With the gypsies gone, Auschwitz became strangely and ominously quiet, as though it was holding its breath waiting for something to happen. I realised that other barracks must also have been evacuated or exterminated, it was too quiet.

No one seemed to know what was going on. Neither Dr Nyiszli nor Dr Mitrovna came to the workshop anymore. The airmen had no idea of what had happened to them. It seemed that they had vanished into the void along with all the other millions of faceless and nameless people who had passed under that infamous arch, *Arbeit Macht Frei*, the gateway to hell.

Late into December that same year two soldiers marched into the workshop with orders to take the three of us with them. We looked at Norman, George and Edgar in turn; they looked very worried and shrugged. They had no idea of what was going on. We knew it would be pointless to ask the soldiers, Auschwitz did not work like that.

"Just do as they say," whispered Norman. "Good luck, boys."

Slowly, we turned and marched out of the workshop. It was the last time that we were ever to see the airmen. It was also the last time we were to set foot in the workshop. We did not realise it, could not realise it, but at that moment our lives were to change dramatically, once more.

The soldiers marched us out of the camp. At the gate, waiting under the sign that promised us freedom through hard work, was a familiar face: a colleague of Dr Pasche's we knew only as the Captain. He told the soldiers he would take us from here, thanked them and watched as they walked back through the gates. I stared at the captain wondering whether he was a member of the underground or not; wondering whether he was offering us life or death.

I speculated idly whether this was to be our 'disappearance.' There was not much we could do but go along with whatever was planned. Perhaps we were going to be taken to another camp. I was sad that I had not said goodbye to Dr Nyiszli and Dr Mitrovna and to the airmen. I thought back to see if there had been any sign from Norman that something was going on but couldn't think of anything unusual. If Norman had known he had given no indication. I was surprised; he always seemed to know everything.

I looked around; the ramp to the station was bleak. Up ahead was a train with soldiers who were mainly sitting on the roofs of the carriages. They were wrapped up in big coats as protection against the cold. The all seemed to be armed. It was the same kind of train that brought us all here so long ago.

The air was cold, it had been snowing earlier, but now the ground was starting to ice up as the temperature dropped. I shivered and wrapped my thin coat closer around my body.

"What is going on?" Erhardt asked the Captain as soon as the soldiers were out of sight.

"I am taking you to the train," replied the Captain starting to walk towards the train. "Come with me."

Erhardt wanted to know if the captain was underground or not. I could see his mind working, he was looking for any opportunities, but no one ever escaped from Auschwitz. Or that was what we had been led to believe.

"Don't worry," said the captain. "Look, the soldiers won't get into the carriages because the Jews have been in there and they are dirty and smell terrible. So they sit on top, pity the trains don't go very fast."

He then dropped his voice and said quietly: "Now, come closer and listen carefully. I have been told to tell you that the train slows down when it gets to the bridge. The three of you must jump. It is the only chance you will get. Good luck!"

He walked towards the two soldiers who were standing at the last carriage leaving us agitated and itching to know more. We knew better than to let any of our emotions show and stood there, eyes fixed firmly on the ground, waiting to be told what to do.

The captain walked up to the soldiers who grinned at him. We could not hear what they were saying but we saw the captain pull out two packages from his pockets and give them to the soldiers. Then he pulled out some cigarettes and they grinned even more. He came back to us. "It's time," he said. "Just remember when it goes slow, just open the doors and jump. You boys have done well. This is the best we can do for you."

He turned and walked away without looking back and we watched him re-enter the camp through the gate, showing his papers to the guards under the sign promising freedom through hard work.

We climbed into the carriage, hardly aware of the other bodies huddled together for warmth. We knew we had to stay as close to the door as possible.

"They are not going to bolt the door," whispered Erhardt excitedly. "That must have cost plenty."

"Will the guards say anything?" asked Mikhail.

"I don't think so," replied Erhardt. "If they are caught accepting a bribe they will be killed immediately. Remember that guard who was caught helping an inmate? He was immediately shot in the back of his head. They cannot risk getting caught either."

Time dragged and I began to worry about us ever leaving. Every sound I heard sounded like the guards being chastised for not bolting the carriage door, every creak was the start of that bolt going through the brackets that held that door fast.

No one inside the carriage spoke. People were too ill or too tired or just too worn out to care much any more. We too remained silent, wrapped up in our own thoughts. It was too risky to talk; there might be a soldier or a spy or someone who thought he had something to gain by telling a guard anything he might overhear. We understood the desperation of the inmates. We had watched as fear, hunger and exhaustion had turned friend against friend, father against son. We had no illusions or false faith in the goodness of our fellow prisoners, or in the integrity of the guards. We knew that at any given moment, the door could be bolted or worse still opened and all the occupants, ourselves included, shot. The different scenarios played over in my mind, each time with the same ending, our twisted and bloody bodies staining red the hard ground. With the gold already in their pockets, the soldiers were no longer obligated. The underground had taken a great risk in doing this for three orphaned boys whose lives meant very little to anybody.

Eventually the train began to move, the door remained unlocked! We inched closer to the door. "When I open the door, jump!" whispered Erhardt, "Don't wait because we might not get away."

I could not believe we were actually leaving Auschwitz behind, escaping from the beatings, the abuse, and the terror. I was willing to follow Erhardt anywhere, I trusted him completely, I knew that he would take care of Mikhail and me. As long as he was with us, we would be okay.

"Mikhail!" warned Erhardt, "Don't fidget! Just stand still and be ready to move. And don't muck up! We won't have a second chance."

Mikhail grinned, "I'll try, I promise."

I took his hand, as Erhardt took my other hand. I could feel the tension in his fingers. He knew we relied on him, he took this responsibility very seriously. It was sometimes hard to remember that he had only just had his Barmitzvah before being taken to Auschwitz. I figured he was not yet 15 years old but he seemed to have already lived a lifetime. His eyes were old and tired. To look into them was to sink into a blackness so deep that you were unsure of ever getting out. I had noticed that very few people met his eyes.

The fingers around my hand tightened and I realised the train was slowing down. I squeezed back and at the same time squeezed Mikhail's hand. We were ready. We listened intently for the sound of the bridge. The rhythm of the train changed the minute it hit the wooden bridge. We edged forward and slid the door open and then stared in horror. The bridge had pylons that stretched up from the water to the sky. We would never make it. We would have to time our jump perfectly; otherwise we risked jumping straight into a pole.

Erhardt clutched my hand more firmly. "Are you ready?" he whispered. "On three. One, two, three..."

Was it luck or were our angels there, guiding us through the pylons, over the bridge and sending us plummeting into the water below? We seemed afloat on the air, hanging suspended between bridge and water. The water seemed so far away. I tried to shout to Erhardt to tell him that I was flying, that we were not going down, but the words remained locked in my throat. I heard shouting and then the sudden rush of air.

Then we hit the water. The shock tore the breath from my body. The current grabbed me and swept me away. I had no idea where the others were, whether or not they could swim.

I heard guns firing and shouting coming from way off. To my horror I saw the train had stopped on the bridge and the soldiers were screaming and bullets were hitting the water all around me. Obviously, gold only bought so much. Swimming was not much of an activity in Northern Germany and I was not much of a swimmer. I was certainly no match for the swift current, which was doing its best to drag me down river, the weight of my clothes pulling me under the water. I gasped, my body strained, every fibre of my being screamed for air. The water was too cold, there was too much of it, my clothes were too heavy, I didn't have the strength. I could see the faint light of the sun high up in the air, dancing on the ripples from the water. I knew I was being sucked under by the current, I knew I was drowning. I could no longer see either Mikhail or Erhardt. The silence was unbearable. I fought, fought the cold, fought the weight, fought against the urge to give in. I knew if I made it, Erhardt and Mikhail would be waiting for me. I knew I could not let them down.

Sixteen

HOW DID WE FIND OURSELVES on the bank of the river, under cover of bushes, miles away from the bridge? Had Erhardt pulled us out, one by one? Shivering, wet, exhausted, we lay there, too tired to talk, too tired to ask questions, our bodies too sore to move.

"Come," said Erhardt, "We have to move. They are probably looking for us."

"I can't," moaned Mikhail. "Just leave me here."

"Me, neither. You go, Erhardt."

"Come on, you have to move, we can't stay here."

"But where will we go?" asked Mikhail lifting his head and looking around.

"We will head for the forest," answered Erhardt. "We might meet up with some partisans."

"Surely they would have had someone meet us." I couldn't believe that they would leave us stranded in the middle of nowhere, without any food or shelter, in the middle of winter.

"They may have had a plan but we were dragged a fair way by the current. Also, there are so many soldiers around now, things might have gone wrong. Anyway, you know better than to rely on anyone else. We have taken care of ourselves pretty well up until now and we will continue to do so.

"Come on, Bernard get up. It's time to move. You can't stay here, you will die of cold, if nothing else."

"I am so cold, I can't feel my toes or my fingers," complained Mikhail getting to his feet slowly. "Please come, Bernard, I need to move to warm up."

Reluctantly I got to my feet. My legs were shaking and I was positive that they would never hold me up. But with a little encouragement from Mikhail and Erhardt I started walking and then running towards the forest. My clothes were icy on my back and heavy with moisture. The snow on the ground was not encouraging. Then suddenly we were within the darkness of the fir trees, their thick branches allowing only the faintest glimmer of sunlight to penetrate.

"Look!" shouted Erhardt pointing to a rocky outcrop. "I think that might be a cave!"

"We are not going in to any caves!" said Mikhail astounded, "There may be animals in there, and spiders and bats and God alone knows what else. Nuh-uh. You are not getting me in there."

"You're the one who used to play with the rats, remember. What's got into you?" Erhardt asked irritably.

"I hate the dark, I hate dark, damp spaces, and I hate wild animals. I am a city boy, I know rats, I don't know forest animals."

I laughed. "Don't worry Mikhail. I am a farm boy. I grew up in the forest. I'll look after you. There is nothing to worry about."

I knew that was not entirely true but figured that it was better to take the chance and get some shelter than to brave the night outdoors in wet clothing. There was always the chance of some dry sticks and the possibility of starting a fire inside the cave. I half remembered camping in the forest with my father, spreading a blanket out on the soft soil, staring up at the sunlight dancing on the leaves. I remembered talks about caves and creatures and wished I had paid more attention at the time.

Apprehensively, we crouched down under the overhanging foliage and began to crawl through the narrow opening. So much for my brave words. I was just as terrified as Mikhail. Only Erhardt showed no emotion, other than a steely determination.

The warmth in the cave hit us immediately. The stale air was deliciously cloying and foetid; it's musky animal-like smell was overpowering, the stench of decaying vegetation was like perfume to our senses so used to the smells of death and human waste.

"Oh no!" whispered Mikhail shrinking back towards the entrance, "Look!"
He was pointing with horror towards the back of the cave. As our eyes became accustomed to the darkness, we could make out three wolf cubs, obviously newly born.
"Don't go near them!" warned Erhardt. "Remember they probably have a mother nearby."
"Let's go somewhere else," pleaded Mikhail.
"I am too tired and too cold and too sore to go any further," I groaned. "Just ignore them and I am sure they will ignore us."
"He's right," said Erhardt. "Here, Mikhail, let's lie down here away from the cubs and try and get some rest. I don't

know where to go from here anyway. If it's a choice between wolves or Nazis I will take my chances with the wolves."

The sand was soft, softer than anything we had known for a long time. We snuggled into each other for warmth. For the first time in such a long, long time I felt safe. I could feel the heat burning through my body. My tongue felt thick, taking over my mouth, filling every available cavity, getting larger and larger until I could no longer talk. But at least I was warm. The heat seeped into my body, seemingly coming from my head and my chest and spreading out down my limbs into my fingers and toes. I was on fire, radiating heat, burning. I was burning too fast, the fire was consuming me, my throat was dry and brittle, I was hot, too hot. I tried to tell Erhardt that I needed to cool down, that he was too close. I wanted to warn him to move away because I was going to burn him, but he couldn't hear me. I was shouting from far away, "Be careful, I am on fire, don't lie so close to me!"

Then I was alone, alone in the cave with wolves swarming all around, bearing their teeth, screaming, telling me that I had burnt their babies. The wolves were howling, calling me a murderer, getting closer and closer, their eyes reflecting the flames that were shooting all around me. I tried to tell them that I hadn't done anything, that it wasn't my fault, that I hadn't meant to burn their babies, but they didn't hear me because my tongue could not form the words and my lips could not shape them, instead they came out as rasping, angry noises that sounded my guilt.

Then everything went dark and it was quiet. Standing in the entrance of the cave a few feet in front of us, head down, teeth bared, was a very large, very menacing wolf. I could see his mate sniffing around the cubs. We did not move, nor did he. I stared at that wolf, he stared at me. I felt myself being drawn into the dark eddying pools within his eyes. I was drowning again in the eyes of the wolf.

Too weak, too tired. There was nothing we could do. I lay there, neither Mikhail nor Erhardt moved. We slept. I think we slept because time passed and I remember feeling refreshed and alive as though I had just woken up from the best sleep I had ever had. I opened my eyes; the wolves were back, coming in through the entrance to the cave. One went straight to the cubs; she had something in her mouth. The other came towards us, growling softly, until he was directly in front of us. We cowered back into one another. Suddenly with an almighty heave, the wolf vomited. I stared in horror, recoiling.

"I think he wants us to eat that," said Erhardt.

"What! Are you nuts?" exclaimed Mikhail. "Are you going to eat that slime?" he turned to me.

"I don't know, I am so hungry."

"Yeuch!"

I reached over and picked up a bit. It was slimy but not foul or smelly. I put it in my mouth.

Well?" asked Erhardt.

"It's fine, it doesn't have a different taste to anything really. Try it. At least it's food."

"How can this happen?" wondered Erhardt as he took a mouthful. "Do you think that God has provided this for us?"

"Mikhail, try it. It's not bad at all. It's not even sandy even though the wolf vomited it up on the sand."

Gingerly, he reached out and ate what the wolf had deposited for us.

"What has God got in store for us?" asked Erhardt suddenly, "is he saving us for something special or just looking out for us?"

"Look at the wolf," said Mikhail suddenly. The wolf was standing at the cave entrance, looking at us and making small noises. "Okay, farm boy, what now?"

I laughed, "I think he wants us to go with him. Maybe he wants us out of his cave."

"Let's follow him and see what happens," suggested Erhardt.

We were beginning to feel stronger now that we had some nourishment and more confident of our legs being able to hold us up. Carefully and slowly, more out of pain and weakness than any fear of startling the wolf, we scrambled onto all fours and followed the wolf through the entrance. Standing upright in the late afternoon sun, the earth glowing orange, I felt amazingly alive, as though I had just woken from a long and peaceful sleep refreshed and rejuvenated. The colours of the earth hurt my eyes in their brilliance. The air was fresh and sharp. I breathed deeply and felt the cold air course through my lungs.

We followed that wolf to a small stream where we drank. The water was fresh and pure, being one of the numerous streams that form in the mountains from melting snow and run in rivulets down to the valley. Unspoilt by human interference there is no purer water in the entire world. We put our faces in the stream, feeling the cold refreshing water washing away all the dirt and pain of the last few years.

I watched it all as though from afar, could see myself drinking at that stream, laughing with Erhardt and Mikhail, and all the while the wolf sat silently and patiently beside us. I saw his eyes, deep and dark and vanished into them once more. I became the wolf watching the three strange animals: half-grown cubs, clumsy and stupid. Falling over themselves, crushing plants that could be eaten, oblivious to the forest, to the earth, to the possibilities of survival. I led them back to the cave, to warmth, to safety, to sleep.

When we awoke there was no sign of the wolves or the cubs. For the first time I had slept without fear, a real sleep, the sleep of the innocent. I felt strong and refreshed.

"How are you feeling?" asked Erhardt. "You had a fever last night. You were very hot."

"I feel great and you?"

"I had the best sleep!" exclaimed Mikhail.

"Me too!" said Erhardt.

"What now?" I asked. "Should we try to find the partisans?"

"Well, we are going to need food and we need to be in a safe area."

We crawled out of the cave. The sun was shining weakly. I judged it to be mid-morning. Half-walking, half running we headed in what we thought was the opposite direction to Auschwitz. Through the forest, away from the river and the railway line, away from the cave, the wolves, the stream, the soft sandy floor. And straight into a German patrol.

They saw us before we saw them. Too intoxicated by the freedom of being on the run, too eager to put as much distance as possible between us and Auschwitz, we never imagined a patrol this far out but there they were, four soldiers. They grabbed us. "What are you boys doing here?" asked one roughly. "We were just out walking," answered Erhardt. "We live on a farm not far from here." The soldiers laughed. "There are no farms near here anymore," one answered and grabbed Mikhail roughly by the arm pushing up his sleeve to reveal his Auschwitz numbers. "Hah! So you are the escapees! We have orders to return you to the camp."

I stared at Erhardt. I wanted him to tell us to run, to hide, to say something, anything. His face was expressionless but his eyes betrayed his fear and sadness. He looked at me and quietly shrugged in apology. While the soldiers were conferring as to what to do with us, Mikhail reached out and touched Erhardt's hand. "It's not your fault," he said quietly. "We were in this together and we did the best we could."

The soldiers were on motorcycles and we were told to get on the back. They informed us brusquely that any attempt at escape would result in our being shot immediately. We had no reason not to believe them. Not knowing what else to do, we clamoured on the back of the three front motorcycles while the last soldier rode shotgun with his rifle ready in case of any attempted escape.

Is this how it all ends? I wondered as we approached Auschwitz. We had hardly gone very far at all. In no time at all, we were being shunted through the gates. Our great escape was over and we had gone in a complete circle. I was disorientated, devastated and confused. There had been no time to talk to either Mikhail or Erhardt. What had gone wrong? What were they going to do with us? Why didn't they just shoot us and be done with it? Oh God, I moaned, what do You have in store for us now?

Seventeen

THEY MARCHED US THROUGH THE GATES, under the sign that promised freedom. The trees that lined the pathway into the camp were suitably barren, desolate and black against the watery afternoon sun. The earth under our feet was soft, springy and grey, quite different to the thick red soil that we had lain in to drink from the stream. The air was different too. The familiar camp smell of death, ash and decay now assaulted our senses after the freshness of the forest air.

We were handed over to two other soldiers, who marched us in a single file out of the gate area, Erhardt, then Mikhail and then me. We marched past the kitchens, along the avenue of trees now bare and silhouetted black against the winter sky, towards the tall chimneys of the crematoria and then past pyres, each footfall confirming that we were on our way to our death. I was frightened, even though I had been witness to so much death, had lived with it side by side every day. I tried to comfort myself by conjuring up images of my mother and father but their faces blurred and morphed into the faces of Irma Griese, Mengele, Dr Pasche, Dr Nyiszli, Dr Mitrovna and Norman. I could not get a fix on any particular feature. I no longer remembered what my family looked like. I knew I did not want to die. I wanted to stay with Erhardt who had taken such good care of me, with Mikhail who had made me laugh so often and astounded me with his kindness. I didn't want to lose them like I had lost my parents, my grandparents, my brother and my cousins. I didn't want to forget their faces, their gestures or the sound of their voices.

"Where are all the people?" whispered Erhardt, turning his head to look at us.

"Shut up, pig!" yelled the guard bringing his baton down on Erhardt's shoulder. I saw him flinch in pain but did not hear a sound escape his lips. Erhardt was right, something was different, there were fewer people around and the camp was eerily and strangely quiet.

They marched us to an area covered by cement blocks. Three cement blocks were pulled up revealing three deep dark gaping holes. I felt the force of the guard's push and then I was falling.

"That's the place for you, little pieces of shit!" yelled the guard. "This will teach you a lesson you will never forget!"

Suddenly the world went black. I felt around me. I was in a deep but very narrow hole. I could feel the cold wet earth close around me. It was freezing cold. I could not move much. I tried to sit down but the hole was too narrow. I could hear muffled voices but had no way of identifying them. Were Erhardt and Mikhail also in pits? Were they alright? Was this the way God had chosen for me to die for to stay in this hole with no air, no food, and no water was surely a death sentence.

I thought of all the horrible ways I had seen people die: the whippings and shootings I had seen first-hand. I had seen boys die during and after the most horrific experiments. We had been witnesses to hangings and other random executions. Perhaps in comparison this was not the worst way to die. But still my body screamed for air, my mind resisting death, choosing life, no matter what.

The air was getting thick and the narrow walls of my grave were starting to close in, I could hear my heart pounding and the noise was deafening. My breath was coming in short sharp bursts. I needed to get out, needed some air.

"Erhardt! Erhardt! Mikhail! Can you hear me?" I screamed. There was no response.

I tried to move up and down to keep myself warm but there was not enough space and soon I was shivering uncontrollably. I could smell my body odour mixing in the rank air, I gagged and choked. My legs began to shake but there was no way I could sit down. I tried to lean against the wall but still that was not enough to relieve the pressure on my legs. I was certain they were going to burst. I reached up and tried to push the cement block but it would not budge, not even the slightest. I had been buried alive.

I thought of all the ways we had escaped death, the experiments, the lakes, the taking of blood, the beatings, the selections. I tried to remain calm. I thought about our escape, and then I remembered the wolves. Had that really happened? I had not the chance to discuss it with Erhardt or Mikhail but I certainly felt as though I had eaten and drunk. I felt physically strong in a way that I hadn't felt for ages. Was it a dream, induced by exhaustion and fever? How does a young boy of around ten years deal with his fear of dark spaces, with wild animals, with crazy adults whose only purpose is to hurt you in new and inventive ways? I withdrew to a place so deep within myself that that boy is forever lost. He literally went out of my mind and it was then that the boy I was, who had hung on so tenuously for so long, finally vanished. I can no longer access that boy, I know longer know who he was or where he went. Too much time has passed to retrieve a sense of him. And in that cold dark and evil womb I was conceived once more, in pain and terror. I revisit that hole in my dreams, for only in my dreams can I confront the horror of that memory. I scream and scream and there is no one to hear my cries. My screams wake me. I want to take that little boy out of the pit, hold him in my arms, and soothe him. I want to comfort him and tell him that everything is going to be alright. I want to protect him from harm. But he is too far out of reach. Time has not healed that wound, although I have waited long enough. Time has only magnified the loss, time has enabled me to get through my day, but time does not get me through the nights. In the darkness, while the body sleeps, the mind plays tricks, revisits old forgotten places, and that boy returns under the cover of darkness, to scream his anger and fear at the world. Time will not heal that boy's wounds.

There was no sense of time in that pit. But when activity began for my withdrawal, it was certainly a different day. My throat was raw from screaming, my feet and legs felt as though they were going to explode. My fingertips were bloody from clawing at the sides of the pit, fighting back – all the while knowing it was useless, but still refusing to relinquish anything. The hole released its hold on me as two soldiers heaved me out by the arms. My legs collapsed under me and

I lay curled on the ground, dirty, slippery and wet, unable to move, blinded by the light of the sun, as helpless as a newborn baby. And those two soldiers that had assisted in this dirty and shameful delivery shouted orders in a familiar but incomprehensible language.

"Get up, pig!"

"You dirty, filthy swine, go to your barracks!"

"You stinking piece of shit, move!"

I struggled to my feet but my legs were too weak to hold me. I saw the raised baton before it fell but I was too pathetic to avoid it. I allowed my body to absorb the blow. The sting of the whip across my back took me by surprise. I had not anticipated that and the shock made me cry out in pain. I saw the satisfaction on the soldier's face; that cry signalled life. Then the beatings started in earnest. I heard their laughter floating somewhere above me, saw another soldier come and relieve the first who obviously had tired of the game. I watched from a different place, I saw my wretched body lying foetus-like on the ground, I saw the soldiers whipping and whipping it. I watched on in sadness.

Suddenly it was over.

"Now get up before we kill you."

"Get to your barracks!"

"Bernard, let me help you!" I heard Mikhail's voice and felt his hand gently touch mine. I struggled back into my painful body and opened my eyes. Instead of the horror of the camp, the anger of the soldiers, fear and death, I saw in his deep blue eyes unimaginable pain and sadness, but also such pure irresistible love and compassion. I grasped his hand as a drowning man grabs a life belt. He pulled me to my feet and together we went over to where Erhardt was lying.

"Is he still alive?"

Mikhail went over to him and gently touched him. It looked as though his beating had been worse than ours. Perhaps they had wanted to know who had helped us escape. Perhaps they had wanted to know who our contacts in the underground had been. Irrespective of what they had wanted from us, what they had taken was far more precious. Barely alive, a quivering raw pulp, the spark of intelligence was finally extinguished. Erhardt's eyes were dull with the acknowledgement of defeat.

"Come, Erhardt," begged Mikhail. "You have to get up now."

The soldiers began to taunt us. They were filled with false bravado, desperately trying to overcome the nausea caused by what they had done. Now that the frantic beatings and the resulting highs were over they had to face the reality of their actions. It was ugly. No one really likes to think that they are capable of hurting defenceless children. They were not sure how to justify it and so kept reminding each other that we were just pigs or pieces of shit. We were nothing like their own younger brothers and sisters, sons and daughters. We were not really human. They would never do this to anyone really human.

We left them to their delusions and somehow managed to get Erhardt to his feet. Then, leaning on one another for support inched our way back to the barracks. The smell, the filth, the cold, it was all still there, still the same. There were fewer people around but there was a strange comfort in the familiar and as we climbed onto the bunk I laughed at our folly. Why did we ever think we could get away from here? Such illusions we had. This was our life, this was our lot. This was what we deserved.

With acceptance came apathy. We lay in our bunks, too weak and sore to move. No one worried us for roll call anymore, no one came round forcing us to work. It seemed that in our absence camp life had changed, or perhaps we were just too ill to be moved. We had all started to cough and every cough that wracked our bodies tore at the fragile scabs of our wounds.

"Why didn't they just shoot us?" moaned Mikhail.

I didn't know what to say and Erhardt remained quiet.

I was worried about Erhardt, he just lay there, coughing and moaning.

"Erhardt," I shook him gently. "We need to organise something. Shouldn't we get in touch with the airmen or something?"

He just stared at me and shook his head and coughed. I noticed with alarm the blood on his lips.

Every now and again someone came with some hot soup for us. Meagre as it was, it was doing some good, for I began to feel slightly stronger. Erhardt was not taking very much at all. His eyes seemed dull and lifeless.

One morning I managed to get up off the bunk.

"How long have we been lying here?" I asked Erhardt.

"I don't know," he shrugged apathetically.

"Hey, you are bleeding again," warned Mikhail. "You probably shouldn't move around."

"I can't lie here anymore. There is so much activity in the camp and no one has bothered to get us for roll call or work or anything. I want to know what's going on."

With great difficulty, my body burning and bruised, I managed to stumble outside. The camp was eerily quiet, there seemed to be no one around. I noticed a column of smoke coming from the main courtyard and went to investigate. A huge bonfire was burning and soldiers were tossing piles and piles of papers into it.

"They are trying to destroy the evidence," said a voice behind me. I turned and saw one of the inmates from our barracks.

"How are you feeling? That was quite a beating you got."

He coughed. Like all of us, he was very thin, but he was also obviously very ill for his forehead was beaded with sweat and there was an unnatural brightness in his eyes. I had seen that look on others just before they died.

"I'm still really sore but at least I can move around. What's going on?"

"The Russians are very close. I heard that Mengele has left. They have been removing inmates daily. Some have to walk, while others go by train. They are trying to clear the camp. The only ones left are the ones like you and me who are too ill to move. They don't really care much about us for we are going to die anyway."

We both stared at the fire for a while, the soldiers too busy to worry about us.

"Have there been any roll calls?" I asked after a while.

"Yes, but only to remove the dead bodies. You boys are lucky to be alive at all after what you have been through."

I walked back to the barracks and told Mikhail and Erhardt what I had seen.

"The Russians must be very close," commented Mikhail. "This whole nightmare will soon be over. Hey Erhardt, maybe we will get to America after all!"

Erhardt said nothing.

I was exhausted from the activity. I lay on the dirty straw

mattress, crusted with blood, faeces and urine and fell into a
deep sleep. I awoke the next morning. I noticed that Mikhail
was also awake. His eyes were wide with terror and he was
leaning over Erhardt.

"Wake up, Erhardt, wake up. Please, wake up."

"Bernard, he won't wake up. Wake him, make him wake
up!"

I wrapped my arms around Erhardt and tried to get him up
but he did not respond. His body was cold and limp in my
arms. He looked asleep. We both knew he was dead; we just
didn't want to believe that it was possible, so we held on,
willing the life back into him. Why had he given up? How
could he leave us? What were we going to do without his
guidance and wisdom? We had once made so many plans.

Slowly, reluctantly, I let him go. One more light senselessly
extinguished by the blaze of Nazism. Mikhail and I looked at
each other. It felt strange to suddenly be only two. Finally I
stood up, took Mikhail's arm and wandered numbly outside
towards the roll call area. "Where's the other one?" asked the
kapo.

"He is dead." I replied the finality of it all beginning to sink
in slowly.

The kapo looked at us for a while and then said: "The cart is
coming along soon, go and get the body."

"That's lucky," observed Mikhail, softly. "Usually you have
to wait days for the cart."

Mikhail was echoing my own sentiments. I think having
Erhardt's body lying on the bunk for days would have driven
us both insane.

We gently picked up his body and carried it outside to the *sonderkommondo* who was waiting there with a trolley. He was so light in our arms.

"What are you going to do with him?" asked Mikhail.

"We are going to bury him. We have dug a huge ditch and all the bodies are going in there."

"At least he is not going to be burnt," I murmured to Mikhail. "He always said it was against our religion to be burnt and that was why the whole idea of the crematoria was so terrible for him."

Mikhail nodded. "I bet all the good angels in heaven are happy. They will be saying to the hoardes of bad angels 'this one is ours, you are not having him.'"

"You are going to have to look after me now," he continued. "And I am going to have to look after you. There is no one else."

"We will just have to survive day by day as we always have," I replied. "I am sure there are some scraps of food around that we can scrounge. I am terribly hungry and my throat is so dry it is burning. We are going to have to remember some of the things Erhardt taught us."

Eighteen

ABOUT TWO DAYS AFTER ERHARDT'S DEATH we were lying idly on our bunks, too weak with hunger and too sick to move. Our wounds were grossly infected, and we seemed to be oozing from everywhere. The smell of death in the barracks was now overpowering with so many dying and just being left to slowly decompose.

At 1 am on 17th January 1945, a sudden flurry of noise and activity around the camp aroused us from our feverish stupor. "Get up," I whispered to Mikhail. "Something's going on out there."

As we ventured outside, snow fell in a white veil all around us, but the ground was black with the imprint of inmates marching to the front gate.

We stood in the shadow of our building, watching and waiting, our bodies still swollen from the beatings we had received, our limbs unable to support us for long.

We saw buildings on fire and heard the yelling of SS officers. German soldiers were throwing papers onto a huge fire quite near to us and, as the wind changed direction, the smoke made us cough.

"What are you boys doing here?" demanded an SS Officer. "Get back inside."

We were shoved inside and the door was locked. We were terrified that our building would be the next one up in flames. In the distance we could hear loud booming noises which someone told us later were the Russian tanks advancing on Auschwitz. We talked for ages about breaking out, but despite our fear, our pain, hunger and thirst, exhaustion overtook us and we fell asleep.

When we awoke we peered through the slats in the window to see what had happened outside. There was an eery quiet and we could not see any activity. Before our involuntary sleep, we had hatched a plan to break one of the slats on the bed and use it to break the ones on the window. Although it took every ounce of energy we had, we managed a hole big enough to poke our heads through. The fire in the buildings was still producing smoke, but the bonfire had been extinguished. A solitary SS officer was leaning against a wall, a bottle in his hand. I recognised his drunken state and whispered to Mikhail that he would soon pass out. As the soldier slid down the wall, still clutching his bottle, Mikhail let out a shriek of laughter.

"Shut up, Mikhail," I gasped, "there could be SS anywhere."

We waited at that window for what must have been an hour, but there was no sign of anyone. We managed to break another slat and lift our skinny bodies through. We made for kitchen block to see if we could find some mouldy bread.

"I don't want any of that sawdust bread," complained Mikhail, "It makes my gums bleed."

"Don't chew it, just swallow it," I said.

The pieces of bread we found were frozen solid and needed to be soaked in water. We cautiously made our way to the latrine, ducking for cover at a sudden noise. We stared in horror as *musulmen*, walking skeletons, moved past us with unseeing, hollow eyes. They reached the latrine before us and tried the taps but the water was not turned on. As we approached they begged us for water and food. We soaked our bread and shared it with them, warning them to take small bites, but they could not bite at all because all their teeth had fallen out. They left us soon after, walking out in the open, uncaring of the consequences.

Eating the small amount of bread had made us even hungrier. We decided to risk a walk to the officers' barracks and mess hall where we had worked before. We could not believe there was no-one around and began to think that we and the *musulmen* must be the only ones left in the camp.

"Do you think everyone else died in the fires?", Mikhail asked me wide-eyed.

"I hope not," I said, "I don't want to be here alone".

At the officers' mess hall we found scraps of bread and cake, all rock hard, but food nonetheless. We took our feast back to our barracks, nibbling on the edges from time to time. With the tiniest amount of food in our bellies, sleep overtook us once again.

The sound of the door being unlocked jolted us from our sleep. The light poured in, blinding us momentarily. When our eyes focused again we were confronted by two soldiers, guns at the ready. They had caps on their heads, not the usual german helmets, and they recoiled at the stench of urine and faeces to which we had grown accustomed.

They did not speak to us, merely motioned for us to leave the barracks and we did as we were told. We learned that there were men, women and children in other barracks who were also being 'freed'.

The soldiers gave us a blanket each and some water, then escorted us back to our barracks to wait for the American field hospital which was on the way. We spent most of that night in silence, lying together for extra warmth, each deep in his own thoughts of freedom.

The following morning we met Chuck, a US soldier assigned to the field hospital which had been set up in a tent outside the camp. Slowly he came over to us and we cringed, expecting at any moment to see a baton or whip, but instead he dropped to his knees in front of us, tears streaming down his face and said: "What have they done to you? What kind of animal could have done this?"

We cowered away and the soldier moved on, but before he left he said, "The Germans have gone, you are free. We have put the water back on and will try and organise some food and supplies. Just stay here and you will be taken care of."

Those last few days passed as in a dream. Feverish, starving, and in constant pain it was hard to tell what was real and what was not. Mikhail and I clung together, adrift without Erhardt, floating in a fog of delirium, anchored only to reality by the presence of the other.

One morning, about a week after the Russians had passed

through, Mikhail and I had managed to get to the latrines for some water, and were sitting outside the barracks. The winter sun was making a pathetic attempt at warming us but it was still better than freezing inside. When the tank rolled up I thought I was hallucinating. I stared, disbelieving, as it stopped in front of us.

"I'm scared, Bernard," said Mikhail. He moved closer to me. I felt very small, very insignificant next to this huge monstrous vehicle.

We watched as a figure clamoured out the top and climbed down. The first thing we noticed was the soldier's uniform and immediately cringed, anticipating the blows. We hadn't been to work in weeks, we hadn't cleaned the barracks or the latrines. We had been stealing food. We had committed hundreds of infractions and now we were going to pay.

The soldier stopped a little way in front of us and held out his hand. "Come here," he said in German, but with an accent we did not recognise.

We slunk further back into the shadows of the barracks.

"Come here," he repeated, still holding out his hands. "I won't hurt you."

I shook my head.

"What are your names?" he asked. "I am Chuck. I am with the US Army."

Still we said nothing.

"Come with me," he said again. "We have a tent set up with medicine for your wounds and food for you. I am here to help you. I promise I will not hurt you."

I felt Mikhail move imperceptibly towards him. Always willing to trust, always believing in the best of everyone, Mikhail could never hold on to any bitterness, mistrust or hatred. I knew he was responding to the kindness in the man's eyes, the gentleness in his manner. I was just too tired, too hungry, too sore and too cold to resist when we were lifted one by one and put on top of the tank. Chuck wrapped a big arm around each of us and shouted down: "Take her away!" I noticed he had tears in his eyes.

We were driven to the front of the camp where a massive tent had been erected. Nurses and doctors were trying to tend to the sick, some of whom were lying on stretchers, others who were just wandering around like ghosts, dazed and confused.

"They are just skin and bone," Chuck said to one of the nurses in the tent, "and they have the most terrible cuts and bruises. They have been very badly beaten. Take good care of them. I will check on them later.

"Don't worry," he turned to us, "they will look after you. I will be back a little later."

Days passed, we were fed, and we got sick again from the food so they had to feed us slowly. Chuck, as promised, came to check on us daily and took over the supervision of our food, not trusting the nurses and other first aid workers. Too many people had died from the food, he explained. He wanted us to survive. The others teased him for his interest in us. "How're your boys today, Chuck?" they would ask. "My buddies are doing just fine," he would reply with a grin. And all around us, people were still dying. Although we were being cared for, we had not escaped that horror. Disease, ever present, now seemed particularly virulent, the stronger we got, the stronger it got. Like an insurmountable wave it threatened to engulf us all. Eventually, when we could hold down our food without getting sick, we were taken back to our barracks. I noticed that they had been cleaned and new straw mattresses had been found. It was the smell of disinfectant that was now so overpowering.

During the day, Chuck would come and pick us up and drive us around. First to the medical tent for some food and ointment for our wounds and then he would take us around the camp in the tank. Sitting on top of that tank we felt like kings. Round and round we went, past the crematoria or what was left of them, past the pyres, the white house, the *Kanada*, the bath house, the infirmary, the quarantine buildings. We passed the dreaded block where they tortured the inmates, passed the wall against which the inmates were lined up and shot. And while we drove we told Chuck everything that the doctors had told us, and he pointed out all the places we had heard of but had not been allowed to see. The stories that the doctors had told had all been true, the details of mass murder and destruction of life, the disposal of bodies, the experiments and cruelty were now made real through the identification of the spaces where they had occurred. Chuck listened gravely, occasionally giving us a hug; sometimes we would see tears in his eyes.

I noticed how Mikhail responded to Chuck's warmth and interest. He was like a plant that had been neglected and now through careful tendering was beginning once more to flower. Broken by the pit and the beatings, battered by the death of Erhardt, I watched as his spirit began to heal. I didn't notice that his body wasn't. I saw the humour return to his eyes, I heard the laughter in his voice. Emaciated, weakened by the onslaught of too many deadly viruses, we were two very ill boys and yet for the first time in years, I felt clean and strong.

I knew I was going to make it.   I would get to America after all.

"Mikhail, we are going to make it!" I would tell him every night, lying on a clean bunk. "It is finally over! These people will take care of us. Do you want to come to America with me? We can become engineers like we said. Mikhail, are you listening?"

One night Mikhail was lying still and quietly. I could hear his laboured breathing. It sounded as though something was loose in his chest.

"Hey, Mikhail," I nudged him, "What do you think? Should we go to America? We can be like Chuck and speak funny."

Mikhail didn't answer. Thinking he was asleep, and feeling drowsy, I turned over and drifted off into a disturbed and disjointed sleep, floating on the rhythm of Mikhail's rasping breath.

The first thing I noticed when I awoke was the silence.

When Chuck came by later I was sitting outside by myself. "Hi there!" he shouted out his usual greeting jumping down from the tank. "Where's my other little buddy?"

I said nothing.

Chuck came and sat beside me. His face was pale. "Where is he?" he said again, this time urgently.

"He's inside," I replied flatly. "He's dead."

"Oh no! He can't be!"

We sat in silence for a while. Then Chuck got up and said: "I promised to take him on the tank this morning and I'm going to."

I watched as he went inside and picked up Mikhail's body.

He was so light, so small.

Chuck shook his head in sadness: "Here is this little Jewish boy who has gone through absolute hell and survived. Why did he have to die this way, when all the hell was gone and the hope of getting out was real?"

He tenderly placed Mikhail's body on the top of the tank and then walked back to me. "Come," he said tenderly gathering me up in his arms and placing me on the tank as well. I allowed myself to be lifted up and placed next to Mikhail. I stared at his lifeless body. I felt nothing.

We drove to the entrance of the camp. "Wait here," he said jumping down off the tank and walking towards the old administrative block. He came out with another officer. They were deep in conversation. "I have permission to bury my buddy," he said to me.

We buried Mikhail later that day. Chuck organised a few of the soldiers and gave him a proper burial. "Why did this have to happen to us?" I asked Chuck as we walked back to the barracks. "Why does everyone I love die? Why did the Nazis do this to us?" Chuck looked away and said nothing.

"Both my friends died in their sleep," I continued, "and were buried rather than burnt. It could have been different. They could have been shot, beaten to death, or gassed. They could have died in an experiment. I should be happy for them, I guess. The angels are looking after them now. I wish I was with them, I have no one now."

Chuck took my hand and gave me a big hug. "Don't worry, little buddy. You still have me. I will look after you. I will pick you up from the barracks every morning and take you for something to eat and then you can continue to show me around and tell me about the doctors and what they told you.

We still have a lot of work to do. I need you to help me understand all this. I need you now. I need you to help me deliver all the food and mail that has started to come into the camp. Remember, we promised Rabbi Hardman that we would see that it was done properly."

Rabbi Hardman was an English Rabbi who had come to Auschwitz with the Allied Medical and Relief team, the same team that had brought Chuck.

The rescue workers had wanted to establish a pickup point for parcels and mail deliveries within the camp but Rabbi Hardman had objected saying that the inmates had suffered enough and insisted that we be treated with respect. To that effect he had the parcels and mail delivered to the inmates and it had become part of our daily routine, Chuck, Mikhail and I, to make those deliveries. Now it was just Chuck and me.

They say that a teacher always comes along when you most need one and that God does not allow you to ever walk alone. Without Erhardt and Mikhail I felt very alone and very cold. Having Chuck around helped but I felt myself giving way to anger, bitterness and hatred. I wanted to kill someone, I desperately wanted to lash out and hurt those who had hurt me. The only problem was that I did not know where to start. Erhardt had always been so wise, and now I felt so stupid, so lost. Mikhail had always been so loving, so forgiving, and now I felt the hardness in my heart, a coldness where once there had been a spark kindled by Mikhail.

Then one day, soon after the death of Mikhail, I noticed a young man who had been an inmate come running into the camp and I heard him cry over and over again: "I couldn't do it, I couldn't do it!"

Rabbi Hardman gathered him up in his arms saying: "What is it? What is it that you couldn't do?"

The man was crying and visibly shaking all over. We gathered around to hear what had happened. In a voice broken by sobs of despair the man told the Rabbi how he had snuck into the village because he had wanted to kill the people who had stood by and watched this happen to him. "I wanted to kill them," he cried, "I wanted them to know the terror we lived with, what they allowed to happen every day. But when I got there, I couldn't do it. I just couldn't do it!"

The Rabbi hugged the man joyfully and I watched in amazement as he began to cry. And in that young man I saw Mikhail. I saw his compassion and his love. And in that Rabbi I saw Erhardt, I saw his wisdom and his kindness. And in Chuck I saw that I could trust again. I knew that there was hope for me; I knew it because that young man had not lost his humanity – in spite of the best efforts of the Nazis he had not turned into an animal. Like me, he had been brutalised, abused and mistreated; like me he had suffered loss and harboured hatred and bitterness, and yet he had hung onto the essence of being human, he had not sacrificed himself for revenge and that restored to me my own sense of humanity.

Nineteen

I AM NO LONGER THAT BERNARD, or as my mother used to call me, *Benoni*. No longer that boy from Holstein County in Northern Germany. That boy laughed with his younger brother, dressed up for Purim, ran between the vines with his cousins Rachel and Leah, that boy no longer exists. The physical and emotional space of my childhood has been forever obliterated and I am left with a jarring dislocation of being. Would I even recognise that boy if, by some miracle, I could go back in time to that pastoral ideal?

With my family gone, and all record of our existence wiped out, with Erhardt and Mikhail dead, there is no one with whom to exchange stories, there is no one to whom I can turn and say "Did this really happen to us?" And yet I have been left with a mandate to tell what I saw. But to whom? For around me I find no understanding, no comprehension of what transpired, only scepticism and fear.

And at that crucial moment when I began my narrative, both language and memory failed me. How do you speak of the unspeakable? How do you remember the unbearable? The spoken word has always been inadequate, unable to convey the horror and fear that we lived with every day, while memory shifts and bends with the passing of time and the acquisition of information.

Here, in Western Australia, on an island off the remote North Coast, I relived the horrors daily in the dredging up of memory required for this work. Was it real? Did it all happen? Was I only eight years old, or older, or younger? Names, faces and places visit me in dreams of curses and whips. They float around my subconscious, tormenting me in their elusiveness, teasing me with half-remembered images. And I want to cry out: "What happened here? What happened to me?"

The things I have told you, they happened. We escaped, twice, we were recaptured, we were beaten, we were experimented upon, our families were killed, and we were starved and treated like animals. We saw people dying horribly, some were shot, some were gassed, and some were starved to death, while others were used as guinea pigs for bizarre medical experiments. All this because of ideology. Because of the ideology of one man, allowed to hold sway over the masses, an ideology that played on the fears and insecurities of the world. An ideology that exploited the fear and mistrust we all carry within us of the "other," the one who is different to us, who wears a skull-cup and black gabardine, or the one who wears a turban, or a veil, or has a different skin colour, or who lives in a different way to the one we consider 'normal'. Nothing has changed, we still fear the other but we have a choice as to whether or not to act on that fear, or to embrace the differences we see. The world is blessed with diversity in nature. It is only in humans that diversity is still seen as a threat.

We always have a choice and it is a simple one, the choice between good and evil. If there is the possibility of a universal truth it is the knowledge of what is good and what is evil. Ultimately it does not matter who your God is, or even whether you believe in many gods or none at all, what ties us together as human beings is our ability to choose between good and evil. The Holocaust was evil, the men and women involved perpetrated an evil, the terrorist who walks into a nightclub and blows up children rather than sitting around a negotiating table is promoting evil. A regime that oppresses a race because of religious belief or the colour of their skin is evil. It is evil because they fail to see the humanity in the other. They subjugate that humanity in order to further their own need for power, they reduce the other to the external manifestation of physicality or practice when in truth those are irrelevant details. What is important is the basic humanity that resides in each and every person on this earth. The recognition of that humanity is the only choice.

I was born a Jew in Germany at the height of Hitler's reign and so I saw things that no human being should see, let alone a child. My family was destroyed because I was born a Jew, my life was destroyed because I was born a Jew and I miraculously survived and like all survivors I was given a heavy burden to bear. The obligation to speak out against the forceful imposition of one ideology over another, of one people over another. To tell the world what happened, not so it would never happen again to the Jewish people, but so that it would never happen again to any people. The Holocaust was a taste of the depths that mankind could sink to, the cruelties that can be justified under a false sense of nationhood and nationalism. Nothing can justify what happened then, or since, for atrocities continue to happen, over and over again. The Jewish people have always studied their past and continue to study and question not only their relationship with God but their relationship with the world. That the Holocaust happened to the Jewish people has given the world the opportunity to take a close look at humanity, at notions of nationalism and civilisation, and question the existence of the grand narratives that made it possible. Unfortunately the world has not yet learnt the impossibility of those all-enveloping ideologies. But we continue to examine the Holocaust, in books, on television and at the movies. We establish theories and philosophies to understand what happened, the effect on the world, how it could have happened and yet even this has not stopped it from happening again. And now the most frightening thing of all is happening: we are becoming immune, desensitised to images of refugee camps, of starving children, of families fleeing from their homes.

It has taken over fifty years for me to discharge my obligation. They have been years of self-denial, years of nightmares, and years of hiding. Nearly sixty years of trying to forget, of not being able to believe that I, a child, not yet bar mitzvah, experienced all that. So many years of wondering how the world I knew could have been so easily destroyed.

Those experiences have left their mark, as much a permanent disfiguring as the number tattooed on my left forearm. But unlike that tattoo I cannot show you and say, "This is what it looked like. This is what it smelt like. This is how it felt." For that I require your understanding and compassion but not your pity, save that for the victims to come, for the day when your children or your grandchildren have the sacred sanctity of their childhood violated, because that day will surely come. The world has taken only one lesson from the Holocaust and that is that there are no innocents in war. The armies of the world have learnt this lesson well. Soldiers, grown men and women, adults who should know better, have hurled their children into the flames, have made sacrifices of their children while the rest of the world has sat back and watched in righteous but ineffective dismay. How much longer are we going to watch our children suffer? Is this pain the legacy we are leaving? What will it take for us to say: "Enough! We will not allow this anymore."

Too many innocents have been thrown onto the sacrificial fires. The question remains: To whom are we sacrificing our children and why?

When Jürgen Albrecht asked me if I could ever forgive him and his country for what had been done to me and my people, I knew that I had to say yes. Anything else would have been unacceptable, not only for him but for me too. Too many people have died holding onto the pain of past wrongs. To not forgive means to offer your children up for sacrifice, to not forgive means to perpetuate the cycle of evil. It is not easy to forgive because we all want retribution; we want the offending person to suffer too. What we actually want is to play God. Our time on this earth is short; the effects of our actions are long. So we may have to back down, to forgive when we really don't want to, to concede what we have built up, but surely, somewhere, deep down within, we know that we would rather teach our children to throw balls than stones.